ADVANCE PRAISE FOR *MIND YOUR OWN BUSINESS*

"Budding businesspeople—and experienced ones, too—will learn more from this engaging book than they would from reading a boatload of business school cases."
—Steve Forbes, president, CEO, and editor in chief, Forbes

"What a terrific book, and what a good thing for those who have worked with and for Sidney Harman that he decided those years ago to Mind His Own Business."
—Norman Lear, television producer and entrepreneur

"Whether the reader aspires to lead a business, a movement, or a nation, Sidney Harman illuminates the path to progress with great intelligence, decency, and wit. He teaches how to be daring without being reckless, how to merge the values of the old with the vigor of the new, how to inspire and nurture a staff rather than control it, how to be responsible to your colleagues and responsive to those you serve. He reminds us that success in business and in life comes not despite our conscience but because of it. A wonderful book."
—Joseph I. Lieberman, United States senator

"Sidney Harman is a true American original. His insights sing a swing with a humor, practicality, and creativity that is always in short supply. We need it."
—Wynton Marsalis, award-winning jazz musician, conductor, composer

"This is not a good book; it's a fabulous book. Sidney Harman has built one of the most respected enterprises in America, and now he writes his memoirs in the same way he leads: with heart, verve, wit, and integrity. Here shines the imagination of an innovator, the soul of a poet, the wisdom of a prophet . . . Every future leader should read and reflect upon it."
—David Gergen, Professor of Public Service and Director of the Center for Public Leadership, Kennedy School of Government, Harvard University; former advisor to Presidents Nixon, Ford, Reagan, and Clinton

"I have never read a book that made business so exciting, so interesting, and so, well, entertaining. Harman's book should be required reading, especially at this time, to restore honor in the profession of management."
—Warren Bennis, Distinguished Professor of Business at the University of Southern California; author of On Becoming a Leader; *and co-author of* Geeks and Geezers

"Sidney Harman's stories of a lifetime of building a great business enterprise make remarkable reading. This is more than a handbook for business . . . it's a handbook for life."
—*Leonard A. Lauder, chairman, Estée Lauder Companies*

"Sidney Harman is that rare phenomenon in American life—the titan of industry who is also a titan of humanity. And, unusual for a business executive, he writes with wit and style."
—*Daniel Schorr, senior news analyst, National Public Radio*

"*Mind Your Own Business* is perceptive, witty, succinct, and vividly concrete in sharing the rich experiences and wisdom of a remarkable entrepreneur."
—*Kent Kresa, former chairman and chief executive, Northrop Grumman*

"At last a book on business (and life) that avoids gimmicks and easy fixes . . . the substance is solid, the stories are priceless, and the writing is superb."
—*William J. Perry, Michael and Barbara Berberian Professor and Senior Fellow, Stanford University Institute for International Studies and former U.S. secretary of defense*

"After forty years in public life, I am now practicing corporate law. How fortunate to have this wonderful book as a guide and inspiration. Corporate governance, marketing, negotiation, and high finance are all reviewed with wisdom, grace, and wit."
—*Thomas Foley, former Speaker of the U.S. House of Representatives, former U.S. ambassador to Japan*

"Dr. Sidney Harman has written a book that Hemingway would praise for its clear, vigorous prose . . . Personally, I wish to hell Dr. Harman had written it fifty years ago. I would have profited from reading it then. But I'm glad I did now. So will every reader."
—*Jack Valenti, chairman and CEO, Motion Picture Association of America*

"At eighty-four, Sidney Harman offers us fascinating glimpses of his long and successful life as a visionary businessman. He adds a valuable almanac of wise and useful solutions on everything from how to get in shape physically to how to create a synergism in your business that gives it the beauty and effectiveness of a jazz quartet."
—*Mario M. Cuomo, former governor, State of New York; partner, Willkie Farr & Gallagher*

"The energy, wit, humor, and brilliance of the man are perfectly reflected in an energetic, witty, humorous, brilliant book. It moves fast and reads fast . . . I was sorry to come to the last page."
—*Beverly Sills, chairman, Metropolitan Opera*

"[Full of] extraordinary insights. Students and practitioners of business, politics, engineering, the arts, and just about everything else will learn what it means—and what it takes—to be a successful leader."
—*Albert Carnesale, chancellor, University of California at Los Angeles*

"Sidney Harman presents a world of widom about leadership in this wonderfully readable book."
—*Joseph S. Nye, Jr., dean, John F. Kennedy School of Government, Harvard University*

"Will inspire young entrepreneurs and businessmen who want to do it their own way. Sidney Harman built a great business from scratch listening to his own ideas and developing his own rules. One of the best business books I ever read."
—*Edward Meyer, chairman and CEO, Grey Global Group Incorporated*

"Sidney Harman is a passionate believer in empowering people. His book *Mind Your Own Business* gives the reader a compass for succeeding in business and in life."
—*Jerry J. Jasinowski, president, National Association of Manufacturers*

"*Mind Your Own Business* is an inspiring book about how to lead from someone who has spent his career breaking new ground—with a moral compass, energetic mind, and generous spirit. The book will change the way you think about the value of leadership, and the leadership of values."
—*Samuel Berger, former U.S. national security advisor, 1997–2000*

"Harman shows us that you can be humane, ethical, warm, and funny and still swim successfully with the sharks, running a model business that is the envy of Wall Street."
—*Norman Ornstein, resident scholar, American Enterprise Institute for Public Policy Research*

"I would make the book mandatory reading in the first month of all MBA classes, take the next two months for discussion, and then do away with the last three semesters."
—*Lester Crown, chairman, Henry Crown and Company*

"Sidney Harman invites us to look under the hood at the evolution of a great company, Harman International. Rarely have we seen a business icon and public servant of such remarkable qualities. There are lessons here for us all."
—*Matthew Goldstein, chancellor, City University of New York*

"With Wall Street and corporate America tarred by financial scandals, fraud, and watchdogs that never barked, Harman's crisp and refreshing little volume, *Mind Your Own Business*, makes a powerful argument that corporate success requires a moral core, and offers Harman's life story as evidence that ehtics work in the marketplace."

—*Hedrick Smith, journalist, author, award-winning documentary producer*

"Open and profound, thoughtful, practical and funny."

—*Andrew Stern, international president, Service Employees International Union, AFL-CIO*

"Sage, apt, and valuable advice on leadership, finance, negotiating, marketing and sales, and most of all, just plain, solid good sense about decency and virtue—a hard-to-put-down read punctuated by wonderful stories and solid insights."

—*Thomas R. Pickering, former U.S. ambassador to the U.N.; senior vice president, international relations, the Boeing Company*

"An authentic voice. You can hear Sidney Harman thinking as you read. This is the book Mark Twain would have written if Tom Sawyer had grown up in Lower Manhattan."

—*Richard Reeves, author of* President Kennedy: Profile of Power *and* President Nixon: Alone in the White House

SIDNEY HARMAN

MIND YOUR
OWN BUSINESS

CURRENCY

DOUBLEDAY
New York London Toronto Sydney Auckland

A CURRENCY BOOK

PUBLISHED BY DOUBLEDAY

a division of Random House, Inc.

CURRENCY is a trademark of Random House, Inc.,

and DOUBLEDAY is a registered trademark of Random House, Inc.

Bulletin excerpt on pages 53–54 used by permission of Bear, Stearns & Co., Inc.

Book design by Bonni Leon-Berman

Library of Congress Cataloging-in-Publication Data

Harman, Sidney, 1918–

Mind Your Own Business / Sidney Harman.— 1st US ed.

p.   cm.

1. Harman, Sidney, 1918–   2. Audio equipment industry—United States.

3. Businesspeople—United States—Biography.   4. Harman International—History.

I. Title.

HD9696.A923U533 2003

338.7'6213893'092—dc21

[B]

2003046295

PRINTED IN THE UNITED STATES OF AMERICA

First U.S. Edition: November 2003

SPECIAL SALES

Currency Books are available at special discounts for bulk purchases for sales promotions or premiums. Special editions, including personalized covers, excerpts of existing books, and corporate imprints, can be created in large quantities for special needs. For more information, write to Special Markets, Currency Books, specialmarkets@randomhouse.com

ISBN 0-385-50959-6

1   3   5   7   9   10   8   6   4   2

CONTENTS

ACKNOWLEDGMENTS

I ACKNOWLEDGE WITH JOY the encouragement—indeed, the persistent prodding—by Jane Harman that I write this book.

And I thank our son, Brian Frank, who added selfless and even courageous criticism of the structure of my first draft. Because he persisted, I produced a far more natural and , I hope, rewarding book.

Barbara Harman brought her English professor's eye and her adroit judgment to a thorough reading and evaluation of what she read. David Clossey read the first draft. He liked it, and urged me to persevere.

Richard Reeves read that first draft and when he said, "You've got a book there," I knew I had to see it through.

Bernie Girod helped me—a lot. He read every word, and contributed to my writing on negotiation and finance. Adrienne Girod read and said she was proud of me.

Bob Feldman made the book his hobby. He fussed with everything, beamed about everything, and he inspired the title.

Roger Scholl first proposed and then edited the book. His enthusiasm, encouragement, and wonderful reasonableness were invaluable.

Karen Cousins and Kathy Baccigaluppi turned my scribblings and dictation into manuscript. No way could I have produced this thing without them.

FOREWORD

I AM EIGHTY-FOUR YEARS OLD as I write this book. I do it because I believe, finally, that the time is right. I had not intended this to be an autobiography, but as it has developed, the book has unavoidably taken on some of the character of a memoir. Still, I feel that my sixty years in business have yielded some valuable lessons about management and people that are worth passing on. Those lessons debunk much of business orthodoxy, much of business dogma.

I recognize that my life would be far less interesting were Harman International a struggling company. In fact, it is very successful, combining sophisticated digital technology and creative marketing with unconventional attitudes and practices. And surprising, perhaps, in today's world, it does so while generating solid profits and consistent growth.

Harman/Kardon, our original division, is now celebrating its fiftieth anniversary. By most standards, that's a long time. I can honestly say that I do not feel that way—not about Harman/ Kardon, not about Harman International, to which it gave birth—and not about me. It has been an exciting, and all too short, journey.

In this book you will find no secret formula for success. You may, however, find it useful as you think critically about what works for you and what does not, what matters and what does not. My hope is that the book will help you generate your own style, your own compass—that it will help you find your own voice.

Ideally it should prompt you to ask, "What do I believe in? How do I use the knowledge of who I am and what I believe in when managing my business or my job?" If the book is success-ful, it will be because of the lessons it helps you draw for yourself.

Through this effort I have learned once again that writing is not the simple transfer of fully formed intellectual inventory from brain to paper. Time and again I have found myself sur-prised, occasionally puzzled, and often delighted at what has transpired. Writing is discovery. It is, as Dylan Thomas said, "the blank page on which I read my mind."

I hope that this book leads to discovery for you also.

CHAPTER 1

SEARCHING FOR SOLID GROUND

*The dogmas of the quiet past are
inadequate to the stormy present.
The occasion is piled high with difficulty and
we must rise to the occasion.
As our case is new, we must think anew and
act anew.*
—*ABRAHAM LINCOLN*

THE STORMY PRESENT

The revelations of corporate misbehavior and financial mischief we've seen recently, and the resulting fervor for reform, should surprise no one.

For decades American business had been in thrall to a pattern of management and development I call, with a nod to Michael

Lewis,[1] "The Old Old Thing." It was the old school of business, conducted by top-down, authoritative chieftains who were for the most part honest, hardworking, frequently unimaginative but diligent leaders. Its characteristics were long hours, specialists as department managers, and profit as the key to success. It was an American ethnocentric world. Global thinking was rare. Other markets were thought of as export opportunities. Technology played a modest role. It was a simpler world, a more realistic world, unadorned by financial magic. One never read of "proforma profits" offered as a distraction from disappointing real numbers. Cash flow was king. EBITDA (earnings before interest, taxes, depreciation, and amortization) was buried in footnotes, if it appeared at all. Earnings after interest, taxes, depreciation, and amortization were what counted. Debt was scorned. The cash register was an icon.

There were significant exceptions: the crazy days of takeover artists and leveraged buyouts, the rash of wild conglomerates. But for the most part, the old verities held.

Then came the cyclone of cyberspace and dot-com madness—a furious breakaway from the old framework. Business was going global, the old notion of export was disappearing, technology was king, and a new breed of high-flying, very young, jet-setting, gold rush, high-tech gunslingers emerged. The so-called New Economy. The laptop, the cellular telephone, and access were the new icons. Pizza hours became the proxy for

1. Michael Lewis's highly popular book *The New New Thing* (1999) extolled the new generation and the new technology even as he recognized its illusory magic and many warning signs.

2

old-fashioned hard work, lavish spending the replacement for prudence and savings. The emphasis was on gratification in the present and earnings in the very distant future. The Young Turks were driven by the opium of technology. Globalization was just a first step on the way to the whole universe. With no real grounding, no personal ethic, no moral compass for guidance, New Economy leaders found it all heady stuff.

Of course, there were a substantial number of creative, imaginative, and solidly grounded companies, but the era was surely not dominated by practitioners of the stodgy tried-and-true way.

Many experienced business leaders were confused, challenged, and threatened by the new breed. Fearful that they would be left behind, striving to catch up, to find footing in the larger world and in the presence of the flashy new technology, some jumped ship for new opportunities with dot-com dazzlers; others abandoned the practices that had served business so well for so long. Desperate to generate profits and the elusive but crucial EPS (earnings per share), some yielded to "cooking the books," a poisonous stew.

THE MAVERICK'S WAY

I have been in business through both periods—for over sixty years. And through those sixty years, I have done it differently.

Let me state up front the principle that has guided me: There is the traditional way to conduct business and do your job, as for the most part it is taught in the business schools and practiced in

3

industry. There is the deeply flawed New Economy way. And there is the maverick's way that looks not to the dogma of the past, nor to existing models of action and behavior, but struggles to determine what is truly effective regardless of traditions and trends. It is a mutant of the Old Old and the New New, a way of thinking that retains the enduring values of the Old and the vigor of the New. One might call it the New Old Thing.

The maverick's way of conducting business forswears the leader as commanding general; it rejects the practice of top-down, authoritative command. Rather, it proposes the leader as catalyst, conscience, and inspirer. It embraces technology, but only in the service of the customer, not to his intimidation or for its own sake. It sees that much of what ails business today arises from the narrowness of preparation, the emphasis on specialization, and the failure to build a philosophical base or sound judgment based on critical thinking. Critical thinking allows one to review business decisions against a carefully developed, carefully honed set of personal values.

When you like or dislike something—a painting, a piece of music, a policy, a point of view, a play, or a business idea—it is useful and rewarding to be able to explain your preference or conclusion, both to yourself and to others. One's evaluations should be based less on "I know what I like" and more on "I like what I know."

Presented with a new advertising campaign, for example, an executive who says "I don't like it" or "It doesn't feel good" may be honest, but this type of comment is not helpful. When you are able to explain your reaction, you will have evaluated and mastered the material and be able to explain why you believe what you believe. For example, "The visual part of this ad does not resonate or harmonize with the text." Or, "The message contradicts our fundamental beliefs," or "The colors are vibrant when the message is intended to be somber."

Developing a reasoned analysis and evaluation that you can communicate to others is the mark of a true leader, a leader who is able to exercise critical judgment rather than one who forces the facts to fit a predetermined conclusion.

You may remember the story of Procrustes (ProKRUStees), a villainous figure in Greek mythology. Not someone you would want to meet, then or now. Travelers on the road to Attica were enticed to stop at his house. Once snared, the victim was tied to Procrustes' bed. Then the poor fellow's legs were stretched or cut off to accommodate the length of the bed—the ultimate "one size fits all." The hero, Theseus, ultimately fitted the villain to his own bed by removing his head.

Over the years, scholars have written extensively of the Procrustean bed and of Procrustean thought—a theory or conclusion forced to fit existing practice or belief. Such thinking encourages the dogma that "this is the way we have always done things." It is the kind of thinking that stifles creativity. Today's equivalent is a failure to "think outside the box."

The leader who sees himself as a catalyst acts in a way that is the very opposite of Procrustean behavior. He may know a great deal about the subject of a meeting, may have more experience and more authority than the others in the group, but he also knows that there is more knowledge and insight available from the group than he or any one person alone can bring to it. The true leader sees his job as setting an environment in which new ideas can emerge that neither he nor any other individual antici-pated. That leap of imagination, that moment of genuine cre-ativity, can only be inspired by the leader who encourages exploration and shows a willingness to consider a totally new ap-proach. In doing so, he promotes the growth and development of his associates and, not infrequently, stimulates a truly original solution.

Non-Procrustean leadership sees the relevance to the busi-ness of ideas, advancements, and events outside the business, and synthesizes them in an effort to make the company stronger. It requires the ability to accept failure, a willingness to acknowl-edge what one does not know, and a readiness to yield to a better idea. At Harman International, I liken our executive team to a jazz quartet in which each player is master of his instrument, but subordinates his playing to that of the group. The improvisation and invention that characterize the best jazz quartets arise from the careful listening and response each musician gives to the playing of the others. It is that interaction, inspired and encour-aged by the quartet leader, that leads to wonderful, even in-spired, music. And so should it be in business.

When the leader is a catalyst, one member, if you will, of the jazz quartet or ensemble, the organization, can change—and a better one can emerge. People have an opportunity to grow and develop, even as hard work and the fundamentals are respected. Meeting one's schedules, financial sobriety, and discipline count, and daring (as opposed to recklessness) is encouraged. Recklessness is acting without consideration of the consequences. Daring, on the other hand, is the conscious decision to go forward after careful consideration of the risks, consequences, and potential rewards. A daring action may or may not work, but it is worth the try. A good leader encourages daring action, and does not penalize it when it fails.

I do not know Bill Gates—I have never met him—and I disagree with some of the tenets of his company. But I respect the fact that he is daring and impressively nimble. I define nimbleness as the willingness to challenge orthodoxy, to question dogma, reject the counsel that "this is the way we've always done it," and to move quickly to implement a new vision. Bill Gates is clearly nimble. He turned the Microsoft leviathan around on a dime when he concluded that the cyberworld was exploding and that the future of his company could not be written entirely in the Windows operating system. His thinking is far removed from that of Procrustes.

Warren Buffett, whom I know and admire, refused to follow the lemmings onto the Net and over the cliff because it did not feel right to him. He just didn't get it. Even as Gates, after careful consideration, determined to chart a new direction for Microsoft, Buffett, after equal consideration, decided against engaging the dot-com world. Though these two friends reached very different conclusions, the process of evaluation, judgment, and action was the same. Certainly each was daring in his own way.

AN ACT OF DARING

My first act of daring, I would say, was joining Bernard Kardon in 1953 to create Harman/Kardon. I quit a well-paying job to start a business in a very new field. A year later we had created the first integrated, high-fidelity audio receiver. Conventional wisdom had it that you could not create high fidelity without using separate components: a tuner to receive radio signals, a pre-amplifier to enhance and enlarge them, and a power amplifier to deliver the enhanced signals to separate loudspeakers. Yet the advantages of a complete, integrated, all-in-one receiver seemed manifest to us. It would be simpler to install and simpler to operate. Because the separate components were combined on a single chassis, the risks of electrical interference and hum would be significantly reduced. So while a high-end receiver flouted conventional wisdom, it made good sense to us. In 1955 we took another major step when I judged that the world of single-channel, monaural sound was coming to an end and that the new world of stereophonic sound was about to emerge. Virtually overnight we abandoned a carefully developed new monophonic product line and created a totally new series of stereo amplifiers—the very first in the industry. They were ready just in time for the 1955 trade show. That decision triggered a huge success and gave us an initial lead over the competition that lasted for years. Decades later, driven by similar daring, Harman International moved early and decisively from products based in the analog domain to products centered in the developing digital domain.

As a result of that decision, we were compelled to seek, excite,

8

and attract a large number of digital engineers. I felt that our way of running a company fit especially well with the new technology. But I was equally certain that we must not subordinate intelligent management and marketing to the technology. Technology must *never* be permitted to tyrannize. It must be the servant of the client. That lesson is ignored at great peril. Many catastrophic business decisions have arisen from the view that the engineers know best; if a new product could be built, that was reason enough to go forward. In my experience, it is not reason enough. The Mazda talking car of some years ago, for example, affronted the people to whom it gave instructions. It was a complete failure. The endless number of self-proclaimed ultimate convergence products for the home, intended to combine all the functions of a computer with those of home entertainment, ignored the way in which people live, and prefer to live. The technology has been in existence for decades to permit the video telephone. Yet people have made clear that they are discomfited when they are observed while on the phone. There is welcome refuge in the telephone's visual anonymity. Similarly, it has taken years for otherwise confident people to overcome their terror at attempting to program a VCR. For many, the flashing 12:00 on the digital readout continues to be a symbol of frustration. Happily, new technology incorporating a hard disk in the home TV recorder does the tough work quietly and invisibly.

BUSINESS SCHOOL THINKING

Business and the business schools have for too long lionized the specialist, the person who has learned how to do one thing and do it well, but who, as a consequence, has almost no idea how the whole enterprise works. Time and again, in small companies and large, I have encountered senior executives who live lives of silent terror. They do their jobs, and they believe that they do them effectively, but they do not have a clue about how the whole enterprise works. It seems to them that the company has a life and motion of its own, and they live in fear that they will somehow be found out. That kind of departmentalized thinking—the specialist in the silo—produces paralysis and an absence of innovation and creativity. Coupled with top-down autocratic command, it is the essence of what I think of as old analog management. It can bring a company's growth to a full stop.

I say, "Get me some poets as managers." Poets are our original systems thinkers. They contemplate the world in which we live and feel obliged to interpret, and give expression to it in a way that makes the reader understand how that world turns. Poets, those unheralded systems thinkers, are our true digital thinkers. It is from their midst that I believe we will draw tomorrow's new business leaders.

Many senior executives, I am sure, decide at some point that they wish to be surrounded by people of similar training, similar aptitude and attitude, similar interests, and similar style to their own. But it is a luxury that, in the real world, rarely exists. Life and business do not work that way. No matter who you are, no matter the company and no matter what its history, in large measure you must play the hand you are dealt. You find people at the company when you arrive, and you promote people as shifts occur. If you were working with a blank slate, many of them would not be the people you would choose to hire or promote. But we rarely work with a blank slate. A leader's job is to lead, to teach and to help shape, to inspire teamwork much as the best baseball managers and football and basketball coaches promote team spirit by galvanizing the players they have been dealt and honing them into a winning organization.

Diversity is a strength. In the ideal company, each participant brings a different set of skills, knowledge, and background, but all share similar instincts and the same values of integrity, hard work, and discipline. It is the job of a leader—whether a manager, division head, or CEO—to meld those different talents into a coherent whole.

A leader must respect and attend to the routine functions of business: the record-keeping, the proper financial restraints, the generation of budgets and operating reviews—the blocking and tackling, as I put it, that were the hallmarks of the well-run "old thing" companies. Coupled with the new processes and new technologies that have proved successful, the traditional disciplines create the "new old thing" companies that will lead the future. A leader must understand the need for balance among the hard disciplines, but he must also know that the soft factors, the human factors, are absolutely critical. If only it were as simple as assembling a knowledgeable management group representing each of the necessary disciplines—accounting, operations, manufacturing, sales—and then watching it work. It just isn't. Psychological needs of managers and employees differ, and emotional responses to the same issue can be at polar extremes. A leader's most challenging responsibility may be to pay sensitive attention to those differences while orchestrating harmony among the members of the team.

The relatively easy part of running a business, I have found, is creating budgets, exercising business controls, managing cash flow. The tough part is negotiating the interplay of personalities and helping them work together effectively. How the leader deals with the temperamental employee who responds to every question or challenge as a personal rebuke, and with the seasoned veteran who strives to keep others at arm's length, is the hard part.

LEADERSHIP IN A DIGITAL AGE

I am proud of the fact that although the four top executives at Harman International could hardly be more different, they have melded into a virtuoso jazz quartet. I do not claim that I have melded them. I have come to see that the best role for a leader is, in fact, to serve as "first among equals," and in that capacity the leader must contribute to that meld. If he is good, he encourages and helps catalyze similar contributions from his colleagues. We have created and continue to refine a balance among the four of us, which is unique. Were the four of us different, the balance and emphasis would undoubtedly be different. Organizations are shaped in passage, and one of the key obligations of a leader is to understand that dynamic and use it wisely.

Our organization is fueled by the nonlinear, multidimensional energy of the group. Although each member brings special and different skills to our work, each encourages the others to be interested in and competent in his specialty—the financial head turned on by technology and marketing, the marketing head quick to respect and embrace manufacturing, and the technology leader sensitive to the way the customer reacts. It is a matrix, a constructive cross fertilization of skills. I think of it as digital management. I am baffled every time I encounter a company working in the world of digital technology but operating and managing in a traditional top-down, linear—what I call analog—fashion. It makes no sense to run a digital operation with old-fashioned analog management.

Because there is no single prescription for success, the leader must believe that it is his obligation and responsibility to work the process all the time—both teaching colleagues and learning from them. Even as those interactions change, they cause the leader to change. It is truly a case of a rising tide that lifts all ships.

Leaders set the example in terms of values and actions, and they must be consistent. Hard work counts. I typically get to my office late in the morning, about 9:00 or 9:30 (our offices open at 8:30) because I exercise in the morning. But I work uninterrupted throughout the day, and I am nearly always there well after our staff has left—and everybody knows it. Bernie Girod,

Harman's CEO, is in the office early—typically before 8:00, and he stays late. Everyone is aware of his passion and his diligence. These things matter. Senior executives set the tone in an organization. Their example counts for a great deal. If the executive has a clean, orderly schedule and manner, and a clean, orderly office, you are likely to see clean, orderly offices and clean, orderly schedules in most other places in the company. If the top executive is disorganized, unpredictable, and messy, that will soon enough become the style of the company or the department.

By conventional standards, my approach to business may not seem very orderly or neat. But I insist that "the whole thing must work," that all of us must see the business as an integral whole. That makes it neat; that makes it orderly. It does not do for a piece of it to function well if all the pieces do not fit together in a seamless, mutually supporting way. When the whole thing does work, it is poetry.

I am occasionally approached by a business journalist or a business acolyte who tells me, "I want to pick your brain." And more often than not, I offer my thoughts. Frequently the person inquiring does not like what I have to say because it does not fit neatly into the framework he is developing. He is frustrated because I refuse to lie on his Procrustean bed. I'm not a collector of others' ideas. I acknowledge and respect them, but I prefer to create my own.

I believe that refusing to accept business orthodoxy uncritically can open your eyes to opportunity. It can serve as a catalyst to inspire your colleagues. But inspiration also requires a moral compass. An ethical approach to business, in good times and bad, is not softheaded romanticism. It is, in fact, hardheaded good sense, because it works.

Among the bright young New Economy adventurers, hardheaded good sense, a strong moral compass, and an ethical base were often missing. How could it have been otherwise? A compass docs not come with the territory. It is principally the product of experience and critical examination. That examination is enhanced through serious and diverse reading and active personal engagement in the outside world—through organized efforts to scrve the disadvantaged (the Peace Corps, the civil rights movement, drives for literacy, efforts to ease poverty or illness). My own critical sensibility was honed by early guidance from my mother, from voracious reading, by teaching educationally disenfranchised kids in Prince Edward County, Virginia, and by the contrasts and contradictions I observed when simultaneously running an experimental college and a traditional business. The existence of an ethical base is not a birthright; it takes hard work and an attentive mind. Nor does it have only one expression. Each must find and cultivate his own inspiration—his own set of values.

The material of a strong, ethical base includes honoring the people who do the work, respecting the letter and the spirit of the law, and believing that a company's responsibility does not stop at the community's edge. Such a base has been my moral compass. It guides me away from the sleek, the cut corner, and the easy path.

In succeeding pages, I'll discuss the keys to genuine leadership; anthropology as the key to marketing; creating products and services that respond to how people really live; and combining old verities with new ideas. I'll also touch on the rewards found in writing, public speaking, storytelling, and humor—generally not traditional business subjects. In combination, all of this can build a vigorous, creative, confident executive and a company that is sure of foot and capable of responding to crisis. In James Baldwin's memorable phrase, a company that "knows its name."

Remember, Procrustes' bed is today's business "box." Get out of bed. Challenge the orthodoxy. Think out of the box!

CHAPTER 2

PASSAGES

Yet all experience is an arch wherethrough
Gleams that untraveled world, whose margin fades
For ever and for ever when I move.
How dull it is to pause, to make an end,
To rust unburnished, not to shine in use.
—ALFRED LORD TENNYSON, ULYSSES

All of us, one way or another, create the arc of our lives. And all of us do it best when we "shine in use." The creation and growth of Harman International has been at the center of my arc.

The instinct for business surfaced in me early. Born in 1918 in Montreal, Canada, the child of American citizens, I grew up in New York City, where there was a candy store on virtually every corner of every block of Manhattan. The owners were usually first- or second-generation immigrants who had cobbled together just enough to manage the rent and the requisite fixtures. Those fixtures included glass-enclosed and locked cabinets that housed the more expensive candies, and a great marble fountain that dispensed ice cream, sodas, and the venerable "egg cream," the joy of New York youth. An egg cream consisted of some chocolate syrup and a dash of milk in the bottom of a glass, pounded into a lovely froth by carbonated water delivered under pressure from one of the nozzles that decorated the fountain. It was the drink of my youth, and the price was right.

It was at that collection of mom-and-pop candy stores that I had my introduction to business. For some time I had operated a growing and nicely profitable newspaper route. First I, and later a team of friends, delivered the morning newspapers to apartments throughout the upper reaches of Manhattan. There were few elevators in that middle-class neighborhood. We would climb six stories of stairs and then work our way down, dropping off the morning newspapers at those apartments whose residents had a reasonable credit history. We would often encounter the milkman as he satisfied orders left in empty milk bottles at the apartment entrances. I admired the milkman. He traveled the streets in a horse-driven wagon and had developed great legs and arms. Twenty bottles of milk in a metal carrier is not a load for the weak-limbed.

I won a number of bicycles as rewards for the performance of my team, and I learned the value of sharing them with my associates. I also noticed that when we dropped off the day's newspapers, there was often a collection of old newspapers and magazines left to be carted away by the building superintendent. With my first real entrepreneurial instinct, I instructed my boys to leave the newspapers but to carry off the old magazines. Then I commissioned a local tinsmith to fabricate some simple metal racks. I took the racks and the now-organized old magazines to the candy store proprietors and struck a deal with them. The racks were mounted inside the entrance to the stores; the magazines were sold "pre-owned but reasonably current" for five cents each, and I split the proceeds with the candy store owners.

That nice little business helped finance my years in high school and paid for my books in college.

I had studied science at City College and business at what is now Baruch College in New York City. Graduated from college, I was hired by Joseph Hersh, general manager of the David Bogen Company, an electronics firm, to work in the engineering department. I remember well Joe Hersh's clarifying comment to the man who owned the company. He had hired me because I spoke English reasonably well. And I remember well how as a kid just out of school I was terrified by the interview. Still, I had persuaded myself that, for totally different reasons, he was too— that virtually everyone is. "Suck it up and do your best," I had cautioned myself. "He'll not know how scared you are." That awareness of the other guy has served me well over the years. Often in situations that would normally cause alarm or jitters—a contract negotiation, a dispute, a golf match—I have reminded myself, "If you're uneasy—if you're scared, the overwhelming likelihood is that he is, too. Each of us is possessed of human frailty. His uncertainty probably arises out of different material from mine, but he's less than totally confident himself. I'm not at such a disadvantage."

Mr. Bogen was, in every sense, a self-made man. An émigré to America from Russia, he had a remarkable facility for identifying a business opportunity and turning a profit. In his early days he had grown wealthy by buying surplus wire and cable from one General Electric plant and selling it, at a considerable markup, to another GE plant nearby. In those days one GE facility had no knowledge of what another was up to, even if it was just a few miles away.

Somehow he became interested in public address equipment and started a small electronics factory on lower Broadway in New York City. It was there, on the fourth floor of the Adams Hat Building, that I was compelled to learn the subtleties of cost accounting and contract bidding.

It was 1939, and America was joining the Allies in the war against German fascism and Japanese imperialism. Hired principally because I cost so little, I soon proved that my career would not be built in the engineering department. Chief engineer Bernard Kardon and I became quick friends, but equally quickly he recommended me to the boss as a management prospect. Although I understood that his real purpose was to unload me, Bernie served me well. I was moved into an office as assistant to the sales manager, a fellow with the perfect name for a purveyor of public address equipment, Haskel Blair. Blair was an older man, an independent sales representative who earned commissions on sales of our equipment to his distributor clients. He served only part-time as the sales manager of the company. I never knew how he was compensated—that was entirely Mr. Bogen's business. The two argued about everything—all the time. But I could compose a letter, and I could do it quickly, and they both liked that. Soon I graduated from carefully proscribed assignments to exercising some control over sales, since Mr. Blair was seldom there. I realized that if I took the initiative and simply did something no one else was taking care of, I would get away with it unless it caused serious damage. Gradually, Mr. Bogen came to detect some modest ability in me and assigned me some of the responsibilities that had been Mr. Blair's. When I began to travel the country in the early 1940s, visiting dealers and selling our products to them, I learned that I had some talent for it. I liked to travel; I liked to study the products (ours and those of our competitors), and I liked to sell them. Exhausted at day's end, I would collect the precious purchase orders I had written, calculate their value, and keep them for a grand presentation to Mr. Bogen when I finally returned to the office. Our customers were radio parts wholesalers who sold service and repair parts to the ubiquitous radio repairmen. Everything was done by hand, and my trove of orders was precious bounty. Over time, as I became more skilled at travel and selling, I became increasingly aware of what the end buyer needed. That prompted me to press for new products when I returned, and often those products succeeded simply because they met those needs. To this day, over a half century later, I can say that no valuable, enduring product ever arose from contemplation in my office—or in the engineering department. It may have occurred there for others, but never for me. I know of no substitute for the firing line, for listening to the customer, for identifying and responding to real need.

There was an annual industry convention in Chicago where we presented our wares in hotel rooms and in the main exhibit hall. It became my job to create the literature, to set up the booth and the display, and to man the room day and night. After dozens of presentations, I was spent at the end of each day, but usually exhilarated. Mr. Bogen would appear occasionally, as would Mr. Blair, but I was there all the time. Inevitably, I was named sales manager and, as I remember it, I began to shave regularly.

A very cautious, very tentative affection began to grow between Mr. Bogen and me even as his son and son-in-law joined the company. I was given the office immediately adjoining his; indeed, the layout required him to walk through my office to enter or leave his own. My sense of competence was growing, as was my interest in a very attractive female I had met. Prompted by thoughts of marriage, and the fact that I was earning all of fifty dollars a week, I summoned my courage, walked into Mr. Bogen's office, explained my circumstances, and asked if he would consider a raise in my salary. He said that he would think about it.

"As long as you are thinking about it, sir, would you mind thinking about ten dollars?"

"I don't have to think about it," he said, infuriated by my impudence. "You're fired!"

"Fired? I don't want to be fired. I love my job. And I'm learning so much."

"I ain't running no school."

I left his office and returned to mine immediately next door. I did more. I returned to work and stayed with it diligently. Mr. Bogen was obliged to walk through my office ten or fifteen times a day as he left his own to walk the factory floor, check the mail, or review what was happening elsewhere in the firm. Not once in the next three weeks did he acknowledge my presence. Not once did he ask me what I was doing there. Not once did he recognize me, although it was impossible for him not to be aware. At the end of that three weeks, I opened my weekly pay envelope. Behold! I was now earning sixty dollars a week.

It was my view then and it is my view now that Mr. Bogen honored determination and respected courage. I don't think he ever really intended to dismiss someone he saw as both competent and a very good bargain.

With World War II changing the character of business totally, the Bogen Company began to build communications gear for the military. I took responsibility for seeking military contracts and preparing our bids. That created new tension between us. Mr. Bogen knew that if we sold the product at a fixed multiple of the sum of our direct labor and bill of material costs, we would make a profit. It had always been so. He had difficulty recognizing that the multiple no longer worked when the bill of materials grew significantly, because the purchased components were built to military specifications, while the labor cost remained unchanged. Use of the same simple multiple would distort the proposed price because the additional material cost carried no additional overhead with it. The resulting quoted price would be unjustifiably high. When we lost the military awards because we quoted his way, he permitted me to bid the next one my way. When it was successful, he fought the next bid and the next, but eventually he yielded.

By the time I went on leave to join the army in 1944, I was a married man and my first child, Lynn, had been born. Leaving my family was difficult. Leaving the company was equally difficult, for I had come to love it.

In the army I was assigned to the Army Experimental Station (AES), a top-secret installation located at Pine Camp in Watertown, New York. Pine Camp was a vast facility that housed the 5th Armored Division. Hidden in a corner of that enormous place and served by its own airstrip was the AES. The United States had somehow lifted the secret of magnetic recording from the Germans and was employing it as the basis for an activity known as sonic deception. It was interesting stuff. The station recorded various dynamic military activities on the magnetic wire and reproduced the recordings over powerful public address systems that threw the sound for distances as far as five miles. The object was to persuade sentries at enemy listening posts that a significant activity was under way, coming at them from the direction of the broadcast, while in fact the real action was developing from a different direction. It was critical that the signal be received through the air at a level just loud enough to be heard—but no louder. The interplay of the information and the sentry's imagination would make it seem very real. Were the signal louder than marginal, it might be recognized as fraudulent. Were it lower, it would not be heard at all.

How that audio information should be developed and, equally

important, how to shape it so that it could leave the mouths of the large loudspeakers we had developed, travel over miles of different terrain, including forests, open space, and water—affected by changes of temperature, wind, humidity, and the absorption effect of foliage—and finally reach that sentry and cause havoc, was the work of the Army Experimental Station. We developed the technology, contracted for the equipment, and trained small companies of soldiers to operate the system and service it in such places as Belgium during the historic Battle of the Bulge, and in the Pacific while at war with the Japanese. It could cause an enemy station to conclude that a battalion of tanks was bivouacking in the south while the real activity was taking place in the north; it could persuade the guardians of an atoll that an assault was under way from the east when, in fact, it was moving in from the west.

I began as a trainee with one of the companies preparing to go to Japan. But it soon became apparent that I was the only military man on the base who knew anything about the equipment. The principal technical work was handled by the famous Bell Labs of Western Electric under contract to the Signal Corps. Their people sighed with relief when they encountered someone in uniform who understood their strange vocabulary. I was transferred to work in the AES laboratory and soon began to teach the theory and implementation of the system to the officers and enlisted men. In time, I was running the lab, and that created a problem. An inspection by the Office of the Chief Signal Officer revealed that a lowly corporal (only one slot above private) was holding the job assigned in the station's table of organization to an officer holding the rank of major. That would not do. But because World War II was nearing its end, senior officers were no longer free to commission new officers in the field. The commander of the station had no choice. He sent me to Officer Candidate School with the expectation that upon graduation I would return to continue my work.

The Signal Corps OCS was located at Fort Monmouth, New Jersey. I was to be assigned there for three months. It was three months of unrelieved madness. At that stage of the war, Officer Candidate Schools were devoted to rewarding enlisted men who had demonstrated long and special service in severe combat conditions. I alone was without any such experience. Although I did not know it, to ensure my acceptance the Army Experimental Station had embellished my qualifications. I arrived characterized as an expert marksman, although I had never held a rifle. I was presented as thoroughly qualified, although I had never marched in formation or filed a military report. My astonishment at my inadequacies was nothing compared to that of the TAC (tactical) officers who supervised the training of the candidates and drove that training mercilessly. I epitomized the army sad sack.

Still, I was determined to make it through. I am puzzled to this day by what it was that drove me. It was not the uniform or the lieutenant's bar; nor did I wish to stay in the army any longer than the army required. It was pride alone that drove me! I began as a clown, ridiculed for my incompetence but somehow reluctantly admired for my determination. I employed every imaginable device to create more time for me in the study hall so that

I could memorize the cavalcade of data an officer was required to possess. I learned precisely what the margin on the left side of a memorandum should be, as well as the margin on the right. I secretly arranged to have the brass buttons on my uniform replaced by gold-plated buttons, so that I would need no time to polish them. I made my cot as tight as a drum and slept on the floor beneath it so that it passed inspection without criticism. I could go on, but the assembly of artful devices and my commitment to that study hall became part of the folklore of the class. The other candidates claimed they did not need watches. They knew when it was precisely 10 o'clock (lights out) because they could see me darting across the quadrangle from the study hall to slip under my bed at night. I made it through, although I came very close to failing on the last day.

Instructions had come down from the Office of the Chief Signal Officer that twenty candidates were to be washed out and not graduated. The administration reached for a quick solution. When night fell, all the candidates were gathered in closed trucks and driven from the grounds. We were dropped off separately along and off the roads of New Jersey and instructed to use our knowledge of the stars and our sense of direction to find the way back. The last twenty men in would wash out.

Now, I have no sense of direction—I need a navigation system in my car to guide me out of the garage each morning and head me correctly to the office. My sense of direction was even worse back then. I was distraught. I did not have the foggiest idea how to proceed. I knew nothing about the stars and was absent any sense of direction, God help me. I have not smoked in over fifty years, but I smoked in those days. I sat and smoked and wept. When I rose I decided that there was little point in climbing up-hill—I would take the easy path down. I traveled blindly. When I encountered a stream, I made no effort to cross it, but traveled alongside. I could only pray that before too many days had passed, someone would come and find me.

Suddenly I heard what seemed to be voices. Scrambling through bushes to check out the noise, I found myself welcomed as third man in. Don't tell me there's no such thing as luck.

After some months at Camp Crowder in Missouri and Fort Jackson in South Carolina, the war ended and there was no possibility of returning to the AES. Second Lieutenant Harman was honorably discharged. I returned to the Bogen Company for another seven years as general manager and heir apparent to Mr. Bogen.

With the war behind us, we were in the early days of television broadcasting and reception. Television receivers were rudimentary and of limited sensitivity. Broadcast signals were line-of-sight. If you were not located within the narrow band of that signal, you could not receive the picture. A new industry erupted to serve the areas beyond that small core. It produced highly elaborate antennas and booster amplifiers to enhance or enlarge the weak television signals and thus provide service to fringe areas.

Those electronic amplifiers attracted many entrepreneurs. Customers were desperate for them, and other companies responded. We did not, although I pressed hard to do so. We were back to the old cost accounting and pricing dilemma. There was no way we could sell those products, the boss argued, at the ridiculously low prices others were offering. "Yes, we can, if you will permit Bernie Kardon to design a product to be tooled and produced in quantity."

I fought another battle, and won another tentative "show me." I reviewed and rated every booster amplifier unit on the market—and every one on the market suffered from having a surfeit of controls. My charge to Bernie was simple. "Give me a booster with one control and we will eat their lunch." And he did. Mr. Bogen screamed, but ultimately yielded. Once we started making them, we never stopped. The company flourished; I was made its general manager. My salary rose, and Barbara, Gina, and Paul Harman were born.

In the early 1950s, Bernie Kardon and I began to have some serious fun. We borrowed a couple of the public address amplifiers and modified them to improve their performance. We paid attention to hum, distortion, and frequency response, and adapted a number of twelve-inch-diameter cone speakers. With turntables on loan from the local radio station, each of us assembled a custom system to listen to our 78-rpm records at home. We loved the result, as did our friends and neighbors.

"There must be a sufficient number of people like us who would love to buy equipment that does what these things do," I told Mr. Bogen. "As of now, they can't. None exists." Once again he yielded reluctantly, and we produced the Models PH10 and DB10 high-fidelity amplifiers. Although they were for us and our times remarkably successful, his heart was never in it. Our hearts were. There were also his son and son-in-law, to whom he intended to pass on the company. I realized that it was time to leave.

So in 1953, Harman/Kardon was formed. Bernie and I capitalized it with a total of $10,000, $5,000 from each of us. Although we did not appreciate it then, we were part of a handful of small companies that became pioneers in the newly developing field of high fidelity. While I have since learned a great deal in my business life, I have no doubt that those years at Bogen were the key, formative years. They had prepared me better than many to build and run a business.

Because our products were altogether new and among the first high-fidelity tuners and amplifiers, and because there were no rules, we were free to follow our best instincts, free to bring totally new thinking to what we were doing. We started in a loft in an old industrial building in downtown New York. Our offices were located right on the factory floor, separated by simple glass partitions. I would walk the occasional visitor around that floor in the most circuitous manner I could, leaving most of them confused but with a sense that there was more there than really existed. And I would airily conclude the tour with the comment that there was little point in visiting the other floors. They were all alike. Of course, we had only the one floor.

In those early days, I visited virtually every town that had a population of ten thousand or more, trying to persuade existing firms to enter the high fidelity business. When I could not, I would assemble a group of six to ten people who had indicated some interest so that I might persuade them that high fidelity was a great, new opportunity. At a small wine-and-cheese-

tasting gathering, I would intone, "Let me tell you how important this is. After only six months in business, we are already the
world's largest manufacturers of Harman/Kardon tuners and
amplifiers." Some would get the joke; others would nod in
agreement, accepting it as a major accomplishment.

It was the heyday of radio, and the big manufacturers in
the field were RCA, Magnavox, Stromberg-Carlson, Philco,
Columbia, Capehart, and Admiral. Each of them produced living room consoles—large pieces of furniture that housed a radio,
a record player, and a speaker. All of them eventually disappeared or barely survived as new technology arrived and
Japanese competition grew. Indeed, signs of decline were apparent even then. The reaction of the "big boys" to the arrival of the
enterprising high fidelity manufacturers was disdain. Columbia
ran a series of advertisements with the headline, "Music for the
99.9%—Music for the 0.1%." The 99.9 percent were illustrated
by a sophisticated family using Columbia equipment; the 0.1
percent by a wild-looking young fellow with wires and a solder-
ing iron growing out of his ears.

Magnavox was the most advanced of the music console makers, with the biggest reputation. Capehart, an Indiana-based
maker, competed with RCA, Columbia, and Magnavox for the
carriage trade. Together they were the establishment, run by traditional business types. Oblivious to the world changing around
them, confident that size alone would preserve their dominance,
they were already the dinosaurs of the industry. They proved
soft, easy prey.

We, the high-fidelity makers—Harman/Kardon, Fisher, Bell,

Marantz, Jensen, Rek-o-kut, Acoustic Research, and Radio Craftsmen—were the upstarts. A more disparate crowd would be hard to find. Among us there was very little sophisticated business management and little experience directly relevant to what we were doing. Some had worked in amateur radio or in conventional radio and television retailing, but for the most part we were drawn to the effort in much the way innocents had joined the gold rush. For all of us, on-the-job training was a necessity. For me, that training was substantially facilitated by two relationships that would endure for a lifetime. Jack Berman was the brightest marketing man in the industry, and Ken Prince was its legendary attorney. Prince became Harman/Kardon's lawyer and my business counselor.

To present our wares, we arranged to produce and promote high-fidelity shows. We rented two or three floors of a New York City hotel. The original venues were the old Taft and New Yorker Hotels in New York City. We removed the pedestrian furnishings from the small bedrooms and set up our displays. Curious about our claims, tradespeople and potential consumers responded to our modest advertising and to word of mouth. The record companies were supportive. Our products were a likely stimulus to more sales, as their records sounded better on our equipment than on the conventional phonograph players the console makers were selling.

The owners of these new, small businesses, including Bernard Kardon and me, set up their displays and manned them throughout the show, and as late as anyone would stay. The exhibitors' displays all looked very much alike. New products hung on pegboard walls or shelves, the principals eager to explain and demonstrate them. Columbia Records would provide newly recorded discs free of charge to each exhibitor. Because they were free, no one resisted, and as a result the latest recording of Richard Strauss's *Zarathustra*, in all its glorious dynamic range, could be heard pounding and pulsing away in almost every room.

Everywhere, that is, except in the Harman/Kardon room. We had no shelves, no pegboards—no fluorescent lights for us. We cleared the room and brought furniture from our homes to set up a gentle, gracious living room with framed prints on the wall, a sofa and club chairs, and soft incandescent lighting.

Where most of the equipment presented for display and sale at the event looked like amateur radio, our first offerings were sleek silhouettes, brushed copper escutcheons on matte black chassis with simple large black control knobs. In appearance, our receivers were more graceful art than busy technology.

And the music! While we loved Richard Strauss and Shostakovich, we decided no conventional classical music for us. Instead, we played Frank Sinatra in our quiet, comfortable room. At the height of Sinatra's popularity, relatively few people had heard Frankie live; most had listened to him on their three-tube AC/DC table radios. Of those who came to "kick the tires," very few spent serious time in the rooms where they could listen to Strauss or Shostakovich. They had little with which to compare what they would hear there. Perhaps the audio was better. It was surely louder, and the din in the hallways was troublesome. But not in our room, HK's room. Almost everyone had heard Sinatra on the radio or in their cars that very day. And how much better he sounded in our room! It was not uncommon for a visitor to demand, "Where is he?"

We were sure that we were onto something. And that something guided the company through its relatively explosive early years. Bernie and his small engineering crew made our beloved babies perform. I saw to it that their appearance suggested that they were jewels—"pheasant under glass."

We all worked astonishingly long hours, but we were in love. I became active in the local trade association and was elected its chair. The group would meet monthly in a New York City hotel. The drive in from our new small factory in Long Island was an adventure because I would always leave for the meeting at the last minute. Last to arrive, I was the first to leave, eager to get back to the plant. Still, if I seemed to work all the time, why did so many of the others get by so well with so casual an approach? Why did they have time to break out cigars and visit when the meeting was over while I was fighting the traffic back to Long Island? It occurred to me that the cast of players I was reviewing came to their roles through an array of circumstance and accident. I would never have the opportunity to observe and evaluate the many who tried and never made it to the starting line. But I should not be beguiled by the occasional fellow who coasted in. There were a good number of them, but they were the accidents and I could not depend or plan on being one. Treat hard work and your smarts respectfully, but recognize that they are neither decisive nor do they guarantee anything. Most of all, I told myself, don't underestimate determination and persistence, and never quit. Abe Lincoln, I reminded myself, ran for the state legislature and lost. He ran for the House of Representatives in the U.S. Congress and lost. He ran twice for the U.S. Senate and was defeated both times. He ran for vice president and lost. Eventually he was elected when he ran for president. The trick, I decided, was to use all my resources to improve the odds. Improving the odds, I came to realize, was the essence of most business activity and most business decisions. Knowing that made the occasional failure less traumatic.

J. Paul Getty once famously said, "The secret to success is to get up early, work hard—find oil." I would paraphrase it for David Bogen as, "Get up early, work hard, pay attention to detail." I would now paraphrase it for myself this way: "Get up early, work hard, pay attention to detail, and fight to improve the odds."

Harman/Kardon was growing at an impressive rate. We had tapped into a genuine longing. The dominant marketer of radio parts, ham radio, hobbyist electronic kits, and public address equipment in the 1950s was a firm in Chicago known as Allied Radio. Allied Radio was the Best Buy and Circuit City of its day, and much of its business was done through its splendid mail-order catalog. Allied's only serious competitor was a small, one-store operation in Boston that produced its own modest catalog. That firm was known as Radio Shack.

When Harman/Kardon introduced its first product line at the summer Radio Manufacturers Association (RMA) show in Chicago, we lit the place up. The senior managers of Allied Radio came by to congratulate us. They were interested in carrying our line. I was invited to the headquarters to meet the president, Abe Davis. A lengthy negotiation followed, during which I resisted what I thought were Allied's excessive demands. At one point Mr. Davis suggested that I borrow an empty office— "Do call your mother," he patronized me. "I'm sure she'll understand." We finally agreed that our line would be featured in two full-color pages in the Allied catalog. For the first time, our products would be introduced to a wide audience. We were on the way.

Those early years established Harman/Kardon as a cult brand. The college campuses were the breeding grounds for a generation who loved the music, and felt that the best way to listen to it was in the dorm with our equipment. Harman/Kardon was the symbol of hip, the mark of the cognoscenti. Even today I hear people tell me, "Hey man, I grew up with HK." In three years our sales had grown into the millions, and our net worth had escalated from $10,000 to over $600,000.

It was then that Bernie Kardon decided to retire. The crazy hours and necessary discipline of a growing business were antithetical to how he wanted to live his life. I was obliged to find the funds to buy him out—and that led me to discover Wall Street. In 1956, Harman/Kardon became a public company, just as the first electronics stock boom was getting under way.

I loved building a business. What could be better? The products were wonderful. They employed technology wisely. They made beautiful music. My instinct for marketing—for selling, for emotive advertising—was not only indulged, but rewarded.

Everything worked. I loved music and found it was everywhere in my life. I loved writing, and found it essential to running a business. I imagined immense possibilities and helped provoke them. I encouraged our people and they rewarded me. I paid attention to the details and that attention paid off in spades.

Nonetheless, in 1962, I succumbed to an interesting temptation. I had encountered an unusual man, Milton Jerrold Shapp, who had built a business in Philadelphia called Jerrold Electronics. The company was the pioneer in the then-emerging cable TV business. It built the first set-top boxes and launched the very first cable system in Williamsport, Pennsylvania. When Milton Shapp suggested that we merge Jerrold and Harman/Kardon, I saw a great opportunity and supported the idea with enthusiasm. The merger was blessed by John Loeb, Sr., one of the great lions of Wall Street, an elegant, powerful investment banker who had a large stake in Shapp's company.

Shapp would be chairman of the new Jerrold Corporation. I would be president and CEO. It was an exciting time, and we proceeded quickly and relatively smoothly to form the new company. As a precaution, we also wrote a buy-sell agreement. If ever we found ourselves in irreconcilable disagreement, we had the business equivalent of a prenuptial agreement. Each would offer a price for the other's interest. The low bidder would be obliged to sell his interest to the other.

Milton Shapp had a personal reason for promoting the deal, he made clear to me. He wished to run for the United States Senate. The merger would free him from full engagement in the business. I welcomed the plan because it promised me a free hand at the new, larger company.

The honeymoon did not last very long. Milton had a way of swooping in without notice, pronouncing his strong views on many business matters. I found the interventions troublesome and inadequately considered. I also objected to his use of company facilities to support his political campaign. As I reflect on it now, I realize that we were both in error—he for a quixotic, even whimsical approach to running the company; I for lack of patience, forbearance, and empathy. He was, after all, the founder of Jerrold, and a genuine industry pioneer. I should have been more tolerant, and when I was right, more persuasive. I should have realized that the employees and the customers were more important than our differences, and that I was putting them at serious risk. I should have worked to find a constructive resolution.

Those differences included one major issue—the future of cable TV. Shapp's view was that cable had arisen to feed TV to folks beyond the reach of regular TV broadcasting. Those fringe areas were where the company should concentrate its effort. I saw cable as serving the cities, the densely populated areas where regular TV could be received, but too often poorly. We brought our growing differences to John Loeb, now a major stockholder in our company, and he agreed with me. That naturally distressed Milton Shapp, who invoked our buy-sell agreement. I was confident that he wished to sell. He was actively running for governor of Pennsylvania, and I was certain he would not wish to be seriously involved at Jerrold. I was wrong. He outbid me, and I was obliged to sell my interest.

Now that I was unemployed, my wife and I drove to the Berkshires to spend a weekend at a small, quiet, family hotel close to the wonderful Tanglewood music festival. I had known the owners for some years as Harman/Kardon buffs, and we were greeted warmly when we arrived. It was evening, and the large living room was filled with guests being entertained by a trio of students from the Berkshire Music Festival. Then I spotted Mr. and Mrs. Bogen among them. It was almost ten years since I had seen him. Excited, I excused myself and ran to greet him. To his everlasting credit, David Bogen looked at me as I extended my hand. "I hear they fired you from Jerrold," he said. Ten years? Hardly a moment had passed.

I invested some of the sale proceeds in the Jervis Corporation, a small, multibusiness, public company headquartered in Long Island. Jervis had operating subsidiaries in Grand Rapids, Michigan, and in Bolivar, Tennessee. I became totally engaged at Jervis, increased my investment, and eventually changed the company's name to Harman International. The subsidiary in Grand Rapids produced modestly sophisticated components for jet engines. Bolivar produced sideview mirrors for automobile makers. I was not very interested in the Grand Rapids activities, but Bolivar excited me because the powerful automakers were its customers. A few years later we sold the Grand Rapids business and repurchased Harman/Kardon from Jerrold. That repurchase began the transformation of the company, and my return to the audio business. In 1969 we acquired JBL, then known as the James B. Lansing Company, one of the world's leading manufacturers of high-fidelity speakers. Harman International was reclaiming a leadership role in the audio business, and over the next seven years its annual sales grew to over $135 million. I thought then that we were getting to be big-time. Today our sales are almost twenty times those of 1976, and JBL and Harman/Kardon remain active units in our Consumer Electronics Group.

In late 1976 the president-elect, Jimmy Carter, asked me to be his new Deputy Secretary of Commerce. I gathered my colleagues at the company and shared the news. Acknowledging an earlier pledge, I said that if they felt the company could not afford to lose me, I would decline the offer. "It is Friday afternoon. Take the weekend to think about it," I told them, "but let me hear your judgment Monday morning. I am obliged to give Washington my answer that day." To my surprise, and deflation, they were back to see me in just twenty minutes. "Feel free to accept," they said. "We'll be just fine without you."

I accepted. Some weeks into the new job, the President's counsel notified me that even if I were to place my Harman stock in a blind trust, my ownership of a majority of the company's equity would place me in an awkward position. Too many issues before the department would present the potential for conflict of interest. I would have to choose between my post in Washington and my ownership of Harman International. I did not hesitate. In the year before I left for Washington, I had rejected a number of offers by the then-conglomerate Beatrice Foods to acquire Harman International. Now I called to indicate that, with one modest qualification, the company was available. The qualification was that I would not be part of it. My lack of involvement represented no problem at all for Beatrice, and the deal was made. Harman became one of its many subsidiaries, and I be-came a wealthy man. I could turn my attention to my new job.

My friend Jack Valenti calls Washington the entertainment capital of the world. As CEO of the Motion Picture Producers Association, he should know. My job was far more concerned with capital than with entertainment, and though it can be ar-gued that the Carter years were less turbulent than these, it was the time of the Iran hostages and of great distress in American in-dustry. Burdened by double-digit inflation and double-digit interest rates, business was in substantial trouble, and the Department of Commerce struggled to be helpful without en-dorsing the complaints.

In 1980, with government service behind me, I was ap-proached again by Beatrice Foods. Their adventure as a diversi-fied conglomerate had been disastrous. Most of their acquisitions had performed poorly. Harman had done especially badly. Beatrice was in turmoil and under enormous pressure from their banks and shareholders. No one at Beatrice understood the high-fidelity business, no one had any affection for it, and the people at Harman were demoralized. Beatrice needed me.

I had an eager seller and, therefore, a very attractive opportu-nity. Beatrice was prepared to finance the acquisition if I would take it off their hands. I did that with only a modest commitment of my own funds. Years later, I realized that the transaction had been one of the first in American industry's love affair with the leveraged buyout—the use of heavy debt, instead of hard equity, to make acquisitions.

At the time I had no large vision for the company, no master plan. I just wanted to keep busy and perhaps make a living. I did instill my personal values about hard work and personal integrity, and my determination that Harman International would be an honorable company. I thought I would stay for five to ten years. I opened a small office in Washington, D.C., and hired Jerry Kalov to move to our primary facility in Los Angeles and run the company. Jerry discouraged my active participation, even as the company was struggling to survive. We agreed that the arrangement was not working, and I promoted Don Esters, who had been his chief operating officer, to run the company. Don and I tried to make it work, but we were increasingly incompatible. I began to wonder whether I could make it work with anyone. I could develop no traction in the company and felt far too removed. Each time I wished to talk with key people, they seemed to be in a meeting. I became convinced that the company would drown in meetings and that Don and I were not an effective team. I am certain he agrees.

In 1992, I turned to Bernie Girod, who had been the chief financial officer. It was a wise choice. Bernie had grown up in Vietnam of French parents and an army background; he was open to sharing and learning, and quickly displayed a facility for engaging others. He sees his role as being a complement to the work of others. While he and I have totally different personalities and different strengths, I was now inside and leading, and I had a genuine partner. And our relationship has grown stronger over the years. The meetings ended, the army of consultants disappeared, and we got to work. The subsequent years have proved rewarding.

At the start I was intrigued by the notion of assembling a stable of relatively small specialty companies, all committed to producing the best equipment possible for reproducing music, and run by people for whom the music itself was important. It promised to be a happy environment, one in which we were doing exactly what we enjoyed. But I knew the fun would not last if we did not pay our bills.

Many companies in the high-fidelity field were struggling at that time. Most had been created by hobbyists who loved the product and loved the music, but were poorly prepared to handle the business activities. We acquired a number of those. They had created substantial reputations and substantial brand awareness—and substantial financial problems. We added Infinity in 1983, reacquired Harman/Kardon in 1985, and purchased Mark Levinson in 1995. The cost for each was nominal. We pursued a similar path on the professional side of the business. JBL loudspeakers had become the audio monitors of choice in recording studios across the country. That and JBL's pioneer role in the movie industry, from the time movies had gone from silent to "talkies," led to a comfortable expansion of our professional activities.

Serendipity brought me to Cleveland Electronics. The company was curiously misnamed, for it was located in Martinsville, Indiana, rather than Ohio. Cleveland Electronics was a subsidiary of the Essex Wire Division of United Technologies Corporation (UTC). Subsidiary is probably a generous label. I saw it as a colony. The firm manufactured loudspeakers for automakers. They were commodity products, installed in the dashboard or door panels to reproduce music from standard automobile radios. Not once in the years of UTC's ownership had anyone from the Essex office in Dearborn visited the plant. All management, marketing, and engineering resided in Michigan. Martinsville was really just a collection of machines and people, and the people were virtually indistinguishable from the spare parts used for the machines. Alienated, and now bought and sold, the employees' spirits in Martinsville were bleak. The day we closed the acquisition, we changed the name to Harman-Motive, and I showed up to assure everyone that we would transform the place. Their understandable skepticism yielded somewhat when I told them that the next morning we would begin to pave the parking lot. The lot was a near-swamp, and the employees literally waded to work after parking. And pave it we did, the very next day.

Since that day, I have been to Martinsville many times. Today it is known as Harman/Becker, and the plant produces Harman-branded, music-reproducing systems for the major automakers. It is a state-of-the-art facility, bright, clean, and superbly equipped, with medical services and a gymnasium on site.

Gregg Stapleton joined the company in 1987 and spearheaded the development of our automotive OEM (original equipment manufacturer) business. Gregg is now the chief operating officer and a member of the jazz quartet I referred to in chapter 1. Together we altered and eventually redefined our role as an automotive supplier.

44

The typical relationship twenty years ago was one in which the auto company buyer would tell the supplier, "Here are the specifications, and here are the delivery requirements and the price. If you are unable to satisfy them, there are twelve other firms eager for the business." In contrast, at Harman International we did the engineering, we manufactured the systems, and we provided our brand as evidence that the system was top drawer. People did not naturally associate automakers with high-quality music systems. When a system bearing the Harman/Kardon, Infinity, or JBL brand was installed, that brand gave legitimacy to the system. We bore little resemblance to the traditional supplier. Car manufacturers could not acquire a JBL, Infinity, or Harman/Kardon music system from another vendor. Over time, most automotive companies moved away from vertical integration. It was much more cost effective to have specialist firms such as Harman handle the engineering and do the manufacturing. We worked together to achieve designs that met both the performance requirements and the cost targets of the car companies. In doing so, we created a new paradigm. Our principal customers were Toyota, where JBL-branded systems were used throughout their range of vehicles, the luxury Lexus line, which committed to Mark Levinson, and Chrysler, which has long been associated with our Infinity brand.

In 1995 we bought the German company Becker Radio, pretty much on the way to its funeral. Becker had been founded fifty years earlier by Max Egon Becker. The company manufactured radios for Mercedes Benz and was, for much of its history, one of Mercedes' unofficial children. Mercedes said, in effect,

"Build the radios, son, and add up how much they cost you. Then sell them to us for that cost plus a profit." In the good old days that worked well for Mercedes, and it worked very well for Becker. But when the Japanese auto companies began to gain market share in the luxury category, Mercedes recognized that it could no longer succeed in the old, patriarchal way. It was essential that the company develop demanding new quality controls and cost structures in order to maintain its role as an industry leader. To its credit, Mercedes changed. But sadly, the old Becker could not. It fell into decline and was threatened with bankruptcy when the banks forced it to present itself for sale. After an intense competition among nearly a dozen suitors, Harman acquired it for a modest amount of cash and stock and the assumption of debt.

We had little concrete basis for the acquisition. The books were in disarray, the customers were alienated, and the employees were dispirited. Still, our fundamental understanding of the business, and a powerful instinct about what it could be, persuaded us that "there must be a pony in that barn." The determination to act on that instinct, the courage to commit the funds to develop the program, the great good fortune in finding Erich Geiger to drive it, and the willingness to take on the giants of the electronics industry—each of whom had had many years' head start—all were essential to feed that pony. That instinct, that determination, that good luck, that ability to recognize opportunity and seize it, and the guts and ability to sell the vision to the bankers, the engineers, the big-time corporate customers, all were necessary to make it work. And it has worked.

Harman transformed Becker and in the process Becker transformed Harman. And we built a very successful business centered on the premium music reproducing systems we were manufacturing for the automakers.

Shortly after the acquisition, I visited one of two Becker factories in Germany's Black Forest. There, a small group of newly enthused engineers had set out a remarkable display. On a table fifteen feet long and five feet wide they had placed the analog equipment—or boxes representing the equipment—necessary to provide music and television reproduction, multimedia, voice-activated telephone, telematics, and navigation, cabin security, weather control, and Internet access in a car. Sitting on top of the many boxes was the wire and cable harnessing needed to connect all the equipment. It looked for all the world like a six-month collection of my teenagers' dirty laundry. Then, on a table less than one-quarter that size, the engineers had placed boxes representing the digital equipment that would provide the same functions. Atop the equipment sat what looked to be a single strand of spaghetti—the "wiring." That strand was Becker's newly developing optical BUS. Employing such technical architecture would make it possible to provide all those many functions at a size, weight, and cost simply unimaginable in the analog world.

It did not require a genius to recognize that I was looking at the future. When I returned to the States, I told Bernie Girod that we had "better find us a digital engineer." Today we have twelve hundred digital engineers in the company.

Bernie, Gregg Stapleton, and I decided that this was the program on which we were willing to bet the company. Our board agreed. It proved a winning bet. Today, Harman International, with over $2 billion in annual sales, is the clear leader in the design and manufacture of all-digital infotainment systems, one of the most important advances in automotive technology in decades. Our systems are, in effect, the central nervous system of a new generation of automobiles, including BMW, Mercedes Benz, Porsche, and Audi. I am confident that others will follow.

Harman International has become the kind of company I have always wished it to be—progressive, able to balance human concerns and technical considerations, and highly successful as it does so. It has proved a marriage of the mind and the heart.

CHAPTER 3

LEADING FROM
THE HEART

The men of old, wishing to clarify and diffuse
throughout the empire
That light which comes from looking straight
into the heart and acting,
First set up good government in their own states.
Desiring good government in their own states,
they first organized their families.
Wishing to organize their families, they first
disciplined themselves, and
Determined to discipline themselves,
They first rectified their hearts.
—MENCIUS, 2 7 0 0 B.C.

Mencius understood the fundamental of ethical conduct. It must arise from looking straight into the heart—and acting.

The ferment about corporate misconduct has often come

close to arguing that the malfeasance is wrong because it has been discovered. In truth, it is wrong because it violates the most critical fundamental of business. One behaves honestly because it is right, because "you do unto others"—because you are responsible for your life and, in your business, for the lives of others. There is no option—no alternative.

In January 2002, as word of the Enron scandal was breaking, I spoke to a gathering of financial analysts and fund managers during our company's quarterly conference call. I think it is useful to repeat here what I told them then:

> I feel the need to comment on the unprecedented accounting scandals and corporate fraud. Some try to explain this phenomenon on the basis that in a large corporation, senior management cannot be everywhere. I reject that notion. While senior managers cannot literally be everywhere, their obligation is to generate a culture of ethical behavior by setting examples and by displaying a sustained commitment to instilling and maintaining deeply ingrained principles of honesty and decency. In my view, this is the central responsibility of management.
>
> I am fully engaged at this company. I pay full attention, and I believe that I and my key colleagues know what goes on throughout it. We run a clean, tight ship. Although our corporate headquarters is in Washington, D.C., we hire and we employ no lobbyists. We hire and employ no corporate PR people, and the only consulting we buy is prudent tax advice. We do our own internal auditing, independent of our auditors, and when we occasionally find a deviation from company policy, we correct it promptly. It is the policy of our independent auditors every seven years to replace the partner responsible for our

account with a partner who has had no prior relationship to the company. The majority of our Board seats is held by independent members. As a matter of policy, we do no business with our independent Board members, one of whom is widely regarded as one of the country's premier attorneys, another of whom is chairman of one of the largest advertising agencies in the world. We do not permit officers or other employees to engage in related party transactions. Our company retirement plan owns 426,012 shares of Harman stock, representing only 17 percent of the plan's total holdings, approximating half of the national average of 33 percent. The only off-balance-sheet transactions in which we engage consist of the leasing, rather than purchase, of equipment. This is an inexpensive and efficient way to finance equipment. Those transactions require Board approval, and they are fully disclosed.

We understand the value of aligning officer interests with those of the shareholders, and we understand very well how that alignment might lead to abuse. We do not abuse it. Further, to present our operations in the most transparent manner, commencing in fiscal 2003 we will account for option grants as an expense.

We know the difference between appropriate management risk taking and reckless buccaneering. We avoid acting so cautiously as to inhibit the company's development, but when we take such risks as investing in the engineering necessary to serve our major new opportunities, we know what we are doing and we understand our responsibilities.

Government can write all manner of legislation and regulation. In the Sarbanes-Oxley legislation, in new SEC regulations, in New York Stock Exchange rules, it has done just that. But all such material only treats the symptoms of the malady. It does not deal with the fundamentals. In the end, trick artists can circumvent the new rules and will surely argue that there should be no further regulation.

In May 2002, the Business Roundtable, the country's powerful association of major corporate leaders, published its "Principles of Corporate Governance." It is a good piece of work. So, for that matter, are the principles published by General Motors, by Target, and by others. So is ours. No matter what these declarations say, however, and no matter how earnestly they are meant, they amount to nothing unless the executives "walk the talk." That, many will do while it is fashionable, but fashions predictably fall out of favor. It is simply not an adequate base.

What is essential is an ingrained, developed, and practical system of ethical conduct. We cannot legislate conscience. It must be the raw material of every transaction, every judgment, every decision. It must arise from fundamental belief. That belief may come from parenting, from religion, from the understanding that it does no good to make money at the sacrifice of one's soul; the source does not matter. What does matter is that the senior executive has no higher responsibility than the setting of the example and the regular exercise of his convictions. And that exercise travels. Nothing is more compelling throughout an organization than the consistent exercise by the chief of simple, straightforward decency and respect for others.

How, for example, can a CEO condone graft in order to do business without realizing that it may well persuade his purchasing agents that taking a bribe is really okay? That's the stuff that contaminates. An honest, healthy company guided by honest leadership is much more likely to succeed in the short and the long term than one that allows and encourages dishonesty in any form. And people much prefer to work for an honest company. It promises security, a sense of self-respect, a basis for personal pride—and it improves the odds for continued progress.

Just as employees prefer to work for an honest company, investors prefer to place their money where they can find integrity in management. After the enormous turmoil of the last year, you can almost hear the sigh of relief, "At last, a company I can trust." Yes, honesty is the right thing, but it is also a great marketing tool. Here is an example of what I mean. On August 7, 2002, Bear Stearns, one of Wall Street's leading and most respected financial institutions, issued a bulletin, which read:

> The issues buffeting the equity market are readily apparent—corporate governance issues, lackluster corporate earnings, questions on the transparency and quality of reported earnings, currency volatility, a valuation debate, geopolitical risk, and fears of an economic "double-dip." What is not as apparent during the darkness of the storm are the investments that will weather the inclement conditions and flourish on the other side.
>
> Seeking to capitalize on the potential rewards of buying great

companies during tumultuous times, we polled our analysts to create a list of investment opportunities that we believe are "Riders of the Storm." Our list is comprised of Buy or Attractive-rated companies that our Bear Stearns' U.S. Equity analysts believe share the following common characteristics:

· Strong, credible management;
· A compelling business model;
· Transparent accounting;
· Improving fundamentals;
· Above average visibility on future results; and
· A solid balance sheet.

We hope this list is of assistance as you navigate the shoals.

I was heartened to find Harman International on that short list, and so were numbers of investors.

In March 2001, when John Mack left Morgan Stanley to become CEO of investment bank Credit Suisse First Boston, he recognized that in the 1990s, investment banks like CSFB were run by egomaniacal personalities who competed fiercely for deals, often at the expense of their own clients and investors. "This firm," Mack told *Business Week*, "had a history of tolerating cowboys." "He is determined," the magazine said, "to return to the days when client relationships mattered more than the promise of higher fees."[1]

1. *Business Week*, September 23, 2002.

To do that, he is dismantling CSFB's star system, forcing executives to adhere to strict codes of conduct and overhauling how the company does everything from issuing initial public offerings to trading and lending—to ensure that its clients' interests come first. Mack is determined to make CSFB an ethical investment bank. Those who fail to collaborate or give clients good advice will be shown the door. He is holding a marathon of meetings to personally tell his twenty-five thousand employees that he wants them "to do the right thing." Harman International turned to CSFB for a major refinancing only after the Mack program was started.

TO WHOM IS THE COMPANY RESPONSIBLE?

Business scholars often struggle with the question, Is the board of directors responsible to the shareholders only? Is the enhancement of shareholder equity the only obligation of the company? Well, who are the shareholders? Are they the investment funds and the fund managers who may hold the investment only until it can be closed out at an attractive profit? Is it the "here today, gone tomorrow" arbitrageur who, as a matter of professional discipline, makes certain to know nothing about the operations of the company and who moves in and out of its stock for profit fractions as he seeks anomalies in the pricing? If the managers are here to enhance shareholder equity, is it for tomorrow only, or for the longer term?

I identify many stakeholders in a public company. The shareholders, of course, but I include the customers, the suppliers, and the employees. The company that treats them all respectfully, fairly, and ethically is a company that over time will survive and prosper—and as a result, will enrich its investors. It may not happen every single time, but once again, the odds are better. And when you know who the real stakeholders are, it is easy to determine who are not.

The financial community may not be a stakeholder, as anyone who has done an initial public offering (IPO) may attest. Typically, the pricing of the stock of a company about to become public is driven by a negotiation between the underwriter and the company. The pricing and an agreement on the "spread" (the commission paid to the underwriter on each share sold) are typically determined the night before the stock begins to trade. Consider that the issuing company is in a very difficult position. By that time, it and its senior executives are thoroughly invested in the effort. Withdrawing over the issue of the terms, although not without precedent, is rare indeed. It is simply too late. And though the issuing company is always characterized as the client, the nature of the business suggests that the banker's primary client is really that group of funds and other financial houses to whom the shares in the IPO are sold. After all, once that has been accomplished, the issuing company is, in effect, no longer a client, but those institutions and fund managers will be the buyers of the next IPO. Whom does the underwriter think of first? Thinking first of the buying institution tends to encourage a lower initial offering price. That makes it easier to sell the issue and is, of course, more attractive to the buying institution. The result, however, is that the issuing company often leaves a great deal of money on the table. It can be damaging to an emerging business.

Nor is the phenomenon limited to emerging companies and IPOs. The very same process applies when an already public company returns to the equity market to raise additional capital. The pricing component is, of course, much simpler. The market sets the price of the new issue; it is the closing price at which the existing stock sold the day before the new offering. But the potent question of spread, the percentage of commission to the underwriter, remains, and so does the pressure on the selling company.

The history of IPOs is that the great majority of the deals quickly trade at a price substantially higher than the original offering price. That history challenges whether the standard procedure is fair to the company or, for that matter, to the majority of its new investors.

After many decades, the practice is finally under review as alternative programs begin to emerge. The so-called "Dutch auction" is one such alternative. Instead of the underwriter establishing the price on the basis that "daddy knows best," the price is set by an auction in which firms and individuals bid for the stock. Thus, the market sets the price and generates a fair, level playing field. Nothing is left on the table; the sellers and buyers get a fair deal. There is understandable institutional resistance to the auction, but I expect that it will become a force.

A company's board of directors should play a strong role. It can and should insist that management summon the courage to demand a fair deal. It can and should insist that honesty be pervasive. Scoundrels have argued (and sadly, many board members have agreed) that the board's control is, of necessity, limited. Neither management nor the board can be everywhere in a large company—especially when the board meets only a limited number of times a year. I believe the argument is hollow. Of course, corruption can occur out of sight of senior management and the board. But the board has no greater responsibility than to select senior managers who are unqualifiedly committed to honest, ethical performance and who know how to build and exercise it. That management, in turn, informs and drives the culture throughout the company. It does so out of a professional conviction and belief that an honest, ethical company is much more likely to succeed. In effect, that management and that board are everywhere.

Better than the Wrong Someone

I am tormented by the executive who thinks that it is his job merely to report on the moment, the problem, or the disaster. I call such folks "weathermen." The executive's job is not to note that it is storming and then throw up his hands. It is his job to recognize the nature of the problem and develop a solution. Weathermen report the event whether it is consequential or not. The report often amounts to little more than "your mother fell off the roof." Weathermen believe that they have nothing to do with the event; they simply observe and report it. The true executive does something about the "weather." And that executive is likely to be well known, not only to his immediate associates but throughout the company as one who exercises critical judgment—and acts.

When criticizing a weatherman, I have sometimes been assured that "the fellow isn't ideal, but he is what we have, and that is better than nothing." I don't buy that view. It entrenches incompetence and deceives the manager into thinking that he has the issue under some control, that however less than ideal, the job is getting done. I believe that in such cases "no one is better than this someone." Removing that incompetent person concentrates the attention and makes vivid the need. Yes, it requires extra time and effort, but in the end it carries the promise of the right person in the job. There are many times when no one is better than the wrong someone.

WHITTLING AWAY WHAT AIN'T HOSS

Although the majority of business chieftains think of themselves in military or sports clichés, there is plenty of room for those who think in creative, even romantic terms. And plenty of room to inform the business with lessons taken from other life experiences. In the late 1960s, my lifelong interest in learning led me to Friends World College on Long Island, where I became a trustee and eventually its president. In my first year as president I traveled through the South with my predecessor at Friends World College, Morris Mitchell.

During our travels we stopped at a farmhouse to borrow the telephone. As we made our way up the porch steps, we stopped in astonishment. An old farmer sat on the back porch, silently whittling a broomstick. As his hands flashed, we saw the most remarkable, startlingly beautiful carvings of flying horses issue from that broomstick. In awe, Morris asked the farmer, "Do you have any idea how incredible what you are doing is?" The farmer replied, "Pshaw—alls I do is whittle away everything that ain't hoss." I have treasured that man's insight ever since. Reducing business matters to their essence, whittling away that which obscures or is unnecessary, has served me well. I admire greatly those who practice the art.

LEADING A BUSINESS

Earlier, recalling my first experience as an entrepreneur, I mentioned the corner candy store proprietors I observed as a young man. They would arrive early, turn the sign in the window from CLOSED to OPEN, walk behind the counter, and wait. During the day they would respond to whatever traffic appeared, and however long the day might go, when it was over the lights were shut off, the sign turned around, and the door locked. That part of life had ended for that day.

I sensed then and I know now that running a business demands a different perspective. Sadly, however, many executives of complex, good-sized companies think that they are running bigger versions of a candy store. That simply does not work. A company requires an articulated mission, a philosophical base, a moral compass, critical judgment, and the realization that it is a dynamic, living instrument populated by complex human beings. A company must forever reinvent itself as it confronts new problems and new opportunities. You cannot simply unlock the door in the morning, survive the day, turn the sign, and leave. It is no candy store.

Business as I see it is a social invention, a small sovereign state. In the year 2001, Wal-Mart's $219 billion in annual sales would have placed that one company twenty-first in worldwide GNP, ahead of 187 countries including China, Denmark, and Saudi Arabia. A company has its own population, and I think of that population as its citizens. It maintains relationships with its suppliers, its customers, its financial sources—and if it is a public company, with the public financial community. It requires a founding vision, a set of fundamental operating principles, and a moral/ethical center. A company is an organism; it had better have a heart.

Leading such an organization is vitally important because so many people and their families are directly influenced by that leader's direction. These are the important keys to leadership as I've learned them over the last sixty years:

The leader leads. He (or she) is not a caretaker. He is obliged to set the targets, the standards, and the example.

The leader defines the company. He should do so explicitly. Its purpose, its goals, and its processes are his responsibility.

The leader inspires. People want work to be more than drudgery. They want to see meaning in their jobs that justifies and warrants the hours they devote to them. Inspiration promises something beyond wages—a sense that the company has a greater meaning, its own values, and its own reason for existence. A leader must find the way to deliver that message and keep on delivering it.

The leader should be the evangelist. Believing in the mission, committing to honorable, ethical conduct, and wishing for creative products in marketing are not enough. The leader must sell those views restlessly and relentlessly. My colleagues and their subordinates must sometimes weary of me. I have often seen that "there he goes again" look. But I have also often seen my influence rewarded, and in turn it inspires me.

The leader must see the company as a coherent whole. It is not enough to be a marketing guru, or a manufacturing or financial star. A leader must see the interrelatedness and interdependence of those disciplines, and must promote the whole of it. Nothing stirs me more than when Frank Meredith, our chief financial officer, embraces an exciting marketing program, or when Bernie Girod, the chief executive officer, engages the central manufacturing functions.

The leader must know that there is no better way to create a family in the workplace than to encourage the family at home. When I initiated a major, new anti–domestic violence program in the company, it was not only constructive in itself, it also enhanced the employees' view of Harman as a caring company, a good place to work.

The leader should never underestimate the value of disciplined, hard work. I am not talking about clocking hours. Years ago, Gary Player, the great South African professional golfer, known for his unmatched diligence, met with journalists after winning a major tournament. Amiably, a reporter commented, "You were very lucky today, Gary." His equable reply: "I notice that the harder I work, the better I play, and the better I play, the luckier I get."

The leader empowers subordinates to do their jobs. He does not insert himself unnecessarily or capriciously. He does not cause uncertainty and indecision, borne of fear of being second-guessed. The leader stays in touch, provides guidance, and, where required, teaching. He empowers, but he does not desert. Delegating authority empowers, but ignoring the delegatee thereafter abandons leadership.

The leader promotes closure. It is important that matters of consequence be driven to constructive conclusion. Many otherwise skilled executives have difficulty making a decision, closing the deal, wrapping the matter up, and moving on. Business leadership includes the ability to recognize that the moment is right, the time has come. If the moment is right, get it done. Finish the job. Wrap it up. The purpose of a search is to find—not just to search. The purpose of a presentation is to sell and get the order, not just to present. The purpose of a meeting is to reach a conclusion, not just to meet or plan another meeting.

The leader knows what he doesn't know. No one knows everything, and the willingness of a leader to acknowledge that he does not know everything is a great attribute. Many outrageous errors are made in industry by people who barge ahead, failing to recognize that they are out of their depth, in an arena for which they are not properly equipped, or because they are unwilling to acknowledge that they don't even understand the vocabulary. In February 1977, only days after I had arrived at the Department of Commerce, I found myself chairing a series of high-level meetings for which I had had no preparation. Those meetings dealt with the decision by the government to expand the 12-mile fishing zone around our borders to the current 200 miles. The meetings engaged flag rank members of the Navy and the Coast Guard and numbers of self-important bureaucrats. I found myself totally bewildered and intimidated by a vocabulary I did not understand. Then the moment came when, suspecting that my inexperience was being exploited, I responded to a presentation by saying, "That was most impressive, Admiral. I wonder, however, whether in formulating your plan, you considered the ADL factor?"

He replied, "Mr. Secretary, that's a splendid question and yes, we considered it thoroughly." I learned an important lesson in that moment. I did not know whether the ADL factor referred to the Anti-Defamation League or to the consulting firm Arthur D. Little. Neither did he. What I did know was that the admiral had been snowing me, and that up until that moment I had permitted a strange vocabulary to intimidate me. Never again. Anytime I do not understand what the other fellow is saying, I ask for clarification. I know that I know a fair amount about a fair number of things, but I never hesitate to admit ignorance, lack of knowledge, or the inability to understand what somebody has said to me. It is surprising how, almost without exception, that declaration leads to a very good conclusion.

The leader knows the meaning of two minutes. I use that as a metaphor. Respecting his own time and respecting the time of associates is important. I have been turned off time and again when someone who has been asked to speak briefly goes on endlessly, indifferent to the fact that there are other speakers or that the audience has its own time limitations.

When I served as deputy secretary of commerce, I was asked to address the Association of Higher Education on the last day of its annual convention in Chicago. I had a very large audience, well over two thousand, and nearly everyone had luggage near at hand, ready to bolt when the session had ended. I shared the platform with the Hon. Willard Wirtz, the former secretary of labor. Each of us was to make an address. I would follow Willard. He started well, but never stopped. As he continued, the crowd grew increasingly restless, and I, increasingly frustrated. When at long last he brought his comments to a conclusion, the hall sweated with impatience. Finally, I was introduced and I told the audience, "Please be at ease. I have a short story to tell you, and then we will adjourn."

Emanuel Celler, I told them, had served in Congress for forty years and loved to tell of his very first year. He had rented the local armory in Brooklyn to report to his constituents. A crowd of some two hundred assembled, and the new congressman began his report. Celler recalled that he became so totally engrossed in what he was saying that "the hours slipped away." When finally the congressman brought his remarks to a conclusion, only one person remained. Celler raced to the man and embraced him. "I thank you for your patience. I thank you for your indulgence. I thank you for your support." "My patience, my indulgence, my support—your ass! I'm the next speaker."

I then sat down. And the hall erupted in the most prolonged applause I have ever heard. Those two thousand attendees cleared the hall in minutes.

The leader teaches. There is no more important responsibility than the development of those around him. There are of course many ways to teach, but the leader must find his way and exercise it constantly.

Above all, the leader develops others. This in my mind is the singular distinction of a handful of great leaders. Lao Tzu, in the *Tao Te Ching*, suggested that "the leader, having accomplished great things, the people all feel they did it themselves."

Mahatma Gandhi is said to have called to his people, "Wait for me, I'm your leader." Gandhi saw the leader as one who promotes the development of others and is always ready to subordinate himself to that purpose. I have known U.S. presidents and others who were downright great when measured against other criteria of leadership, but who failed seriously in this respect. Most leaders think a great deal about their legacy. What greater legacy than a group of followers or colleagues who carry on, inspired, informed, and grown because of the relationship with their leader?

The very best leaders go beyond the mere setting of example. The best leaders are catalysts who prompt others to reach beyond their most natural abilities to find something they had previously thought beyond their reach. The routine leader causes nothing to emerge from a meeting except those ideas which the participants brought with them. The catalyst/leader will frequently cause a leap of imagination—a leap of faith, the discovery of something no one had brought to the meeting.

The leader recognizes that people are often at their very best the moment they have been let go. That used to puzzle me. Have I made an error in judgment? How can this fellow look this good and yet have persuaded me that he cannot cut it? With enough experience, I have come to realize that people frequently do badly because they hate the work or are overwhelmed by the responsibility, or because they are terrified because they do not understand how the whole thing works. They are released from that dreadful struggle at the moment of dismissal, and with that release, are free to perform at their very best. It took more than one experience for me to realize that it should not seduce me into changing my mind. Each time I did, I was soon obliged to act all over again.

I learned a great deal about leadership from Mr. Bogen, my first and only business boss. I observed him with a combination of curiosity, admiration, attention, and growing frustration. He was always aware of everything—every detail. He gave diligence a very good name. He devoted Saturday to the adding machine. I would come into work and find him in the accounting office, personally cranking out every receipt, every invoice—all the billing. He knew where the pulse of the business was and never took his finger off it. I came to respect the importance of attention to detail. I've never lost it.

I also learned plenty about how to relate to employees. Mr. Bogen possessed a great eye for opportunity and a great love for detail and dialogue, but a deaf ear and a fundamental insensitivity to people. There was the fateful day when our green-eyeshade bookkeeper arrived thirty minutes late. That was no ordinary event. Terrified of the boss, the bookkeeper was always the first employee to arrive. Yet on that day, he was not only thirty minutes late, but bleeding from a head wound, his clothes torn and dirty.

"I am so sorry," he offered as he staggered from the elevator to a sharp-eyed reception. "I left for work early, but a group of ruffians threw me down three flights of subway steps." After a brief pause, Mr. Bogen responded, "Three flights of steps don't take thirty minutes."

As I reflect on those formative years, I realize that we often learn as much by recognizing what is negative as we do by recognizing what is positive in our teachers. For all his severity, for all his mistrust of people and sophisticated accounting practices, Mr. Bogen was the most intuitive, most decisive businessman I have ever met.

He was not a man for big ideas, but nowhere else could I have learned the value in mastering detail. Today I am convinced that the familiar argument over whether a leader should be a man of vision or one who pays attention to detail is spurious. I am convinced that the true leader combines the two. A bear for detail who has no heart or scope will run a dull, desultory business. The person of grand vision who has little idea or interest in how to exercise it will leave disaster in his wake.

Mr. Bogen was a powerful influence in my life as I constantly combed through the positives and negatives of the man. I still remember his habit of tying a knot in his handkerchief to remind himself of something. He did not need to note the specific of the matter, only to be reminded that he had something that needed attention. I'm not that good. I stuff the pocket of my shirt with notes reminding me of things I must attend to, but also of ideas that I must find time to explore. They tumble out of my pocket at night even as those wonderful orders, written by hand at the distributor's desk and lovingly collected each day, tumbled out on the bed of my hotel room each night of my early days on the road.

When you run a business, you never leave it. You never approach the day as something merely to get through—something to get behind you. Each day is a new adventure, a new experience, and a new challenge. If the business lives—then so do you.

I take for granted that each of us brings technical skills to our work, and I know that there are many books dealing with such material. I am certain that my engineering and social psychology training have been useful to me. But for now I take that stuff for granted. Here, I deal with other factors that no one should take for granted.

When I walk the floors of our factories, I spend much of the time speaking to the people who do the work. I always learn from it, and they always draw the correct inference, that I care about them. It is folklore in the company that "the old man" never walks the floor without checking the labels on the shipping cartons and without straightening the pictures or signs on the walls. That is not mere idiosyncrasy. I am convinced that if the label on a carton is crooked, it speaks to a state of mind. If the label is crooked, I question the quality of the contents of the carton. And I know that as I fuss with that kind of thing, it earns me the sometimes amused but always appreciative respect of the people on the line.

No matter the level at which the executive works, scanning all of the operations is a vital tool. It may seem self-evident, but it is all too rarely practiced. By scanning, I mean to review each operation, aware that none is a simple candy store, that each unit experiences its own dynamic, reflecting changes in the marketplace, in the technology, and in its people. That, therefore, it cannot be assumed that it stands in place, unchanged from the previous review.

I have found that scanning is facilitated by requiring each operating unit manager to write a monthly report. The report always includes a full profit and loss statement and balance sheet that I review thoroughly, but it is the commentary that is crucial.

In that commentary, I ask the reporting manager to review his unit and identify the critical changes, influences, problems, and opportunities. This requirement encourages the very writing in business that I will promote later in this book, and it invariably reveals the way in which the manager thinks. By avoiding a standard form of report, I leave it to each manager to discover his own style and his own way of processing the material. It tells me a lot about the manager, and it can tell the manager a lot about himself.

I prepare my own monthly report for the members of our board. It follows the same pattern. Each report I write includes full financial documentation for the period, but then I engage the reader in the significant aspects of the business. In effect, I walk each director through the raw material of the company—its achievements and its opportunities, its successes and its disappointments. Our board members frequently tell me that they feel very close to the business because the monthly reports give them the sense of an uninterrupted, continuous board meeting.

Many firms farm out the creation of the annual report to advertising agencies or annual report specialists. We don't. We write every word of our annual report, and I am its principal author. I believe that if the manager of a company cannot summon an authentic voice to review and evaluate company operations for the year, that manager should find himself a new day job. It is not only right for the shareholders to hear an authentic voice, it is also excellent discipline for the manager who writes his own report. I have been told by shareholders and analysts that they

71

read our reports because they are straightforward, informative, and credible. I think that's good. It also costs a great deal less to produce a report that way.

Corporate press releases, annual reports, and company brochures often declare that "people are our primary asset." Unless that precious sentiment is combined with programs that reflect it, it is both precious and empty. Over the years I have learned that dignity on the shop floor is the foundation on which to build constructive processes. Dignity begins with recognizing the aspirations, the needs, and the creative and productive capacities of working people. Years ago we calculated the investment in training and preparation the company made in all of its workers, and realized quickly how inefficient and costly (as well as uncaring) the drive to downsize through job elimination can be.

From time to time we have been compelled to reduce our labor force. We never do it without that thorough analysis. Most times we have found that we could develop other opportunities for the affected employees within the same plant or at other of our facilities. Equally important, we have learned how costly it is to reduce a workforce and then rehire new people when things pick up. We know that it is not weakness or softheadedness to see the reductions as a last resort. In the net, a wise delay often saves a great deal of money. It always pays in employee awareness and support.

The Executive Chairman and Succession

My title is Harman International's executive chairman. It is a title widely employed in Europe but only beginning to be used in
the United States. It distinguishes between the chairman who
works full-time and is totally involved in all company operations
from one who appears only at board meetings with the other
members. Ours is a small board. There are three inside and four
independent directors. The independent directors (half of them
are female) serve on each of the committees of the board, including compensation, audit, corporate governance, and nominat-
ing. I have heard on occasion that for a company of our size, it is
a small board. I do not think that the number of bodies is important. It is important that each member brings a special personal
history and set of talents that enrich the board meetings and assure seasoned and balanced consideration. Our directors are
informed participants, responsible for the oversight of the business.

Over the years I have emphasized to the board members that
they have no greater responsibility than the selection and continuing evaluation of the top officers of the company. That surely
includes me, and I am, I acknowledge, a somewhat special case.
I founded this company and I am chronologically threatened.
Am I perhaps too old? Have I lost a critical step? Will I recognize
that the time has come to step aside? I have suggested that the
least likely person to make that judgment is the man himself.
Rarely, if ever, does the principal executive, the star athlete, or
the star performer recognize when that moment has come. The

board has the responsibility to make that evaluation, but it has an equal responsibility not to force departure when the person is making a significant contribution—not to force departure simply because of the calendar.

From time to time in recent years, members of the financial community have raised the same subject by politely asking about succession. It is a totally legitimate inquiry, but I am amused to realize that since that day in 1998 when the board recognized Bernie Girod as vice chairman and CEO and me as executive chairman, there has not been a single question about succession. Nothing changed in the way the company operates or is managed—nothing, that is, except the titles. I suppose the reason for the response is that the board's action suggested that it is not now required to think about succession; it has already taken care of the matter. Our CEO is in place and is happy with the arrangement, in which I continue as "first among equals." If he is happy, the board is happy, the community is happy, and I am happy.

We bring the same thinking to the question of mandatory retirement. For what it's worth, I regard that as one of the sillier constructs in business management. I understand that it is intended to facilitate the transition from older management to younger, so-called "fresh blood." Not infrequently, it provides a gracious way to remove someone who has stayed beyond his time. But it can also result in the departure of rare and valuable talent. The calendar is not a thoughtful judge. It is mechanical and arbitrary, and I believe that it should not relieve the board of a key responsibility: to judge the talent as you find it and act clinically to move it out if and when it cannot do the job—regardless of age. As I write this, I know it is self-serving, but I am comfortable with the conviction that I am fooling no one, and that when I lose that important step, the board will know it and the board will act—if I don't beat them to it.

CHAPTER 4

THE BUZZER WORKS FOR ME

*If at first
the idea is not absurd,
then there is no hope for it.*
—*ALBERT EINSTEIN*

In 1970, I was living a strangely bifurcated life. I was running Harman International full-time, and I was deeply involved at Friends World College. FWC was one of a number of institutions of higher learning formed or sponsored by the Society of Friends, the Quakers. In 1970, I had moved from serving as a member of the board of the college to serving as its full-time president. To manage both the business and the college, I would be in my office at Harman International as early as 7:00 or 7:30 in the morning. In the afternoon I would eat a brown-bag lunch while driving myself from the office in Lake Success to the Long Island campus of the college, twenty-five minutes away. Arriving at 2:00 or 3:00 P.M., I would change in the car from my suit into the uniform of academic life, jeans and an open shirt. I was usually there until 11:00 P.M. The days were lengthy and taxing, but the pace and intellectual stimuli filled me with excitement.

With educational centers around the world, FWC operated with the conviction that young people learn best when they take responsibility for their own education. This view contradicted educational tradition, which held that teachers possessed the knowledge and information students needed, and that it was their responsibility to somehow deliver it to the students. Friends World College viewed the teacher as a resource rather than as the unchallenged fountainhead. The college looked to the student to design and execute his or her study program. When it worked, the student learned well and widely, and developed a strong sense of personal responsibility. At its best, it was the embodiment of Horace Mann's metaphor of the student and the teacher on a log, teaching and learning. From a distance, an observer would not be able to tell who was the teacher and who the student. Each taught, and learned from, the other. The effect could be electrifying, and I was often the most stimulated on the campus.

Although I believed that I was supervising an important new experiment in American education, I failed to recognize that, at the same time, in my business life I was running a traditional, autocratic, top-down company. Somehow I had not recognized the disconnect between what I was learning about supervision and responsibility at the college, and the very different way I supervised and managed my employees.

All of that changed dramatically because of a disruption in our Bolivar, Tennessee, plant. It was in Bolivar that our subsidiary, Harman Automotive, manufactured remote-controlled side-view mirrors for the automakers. Bolivar is a small town fifty miles northeast of Memphis. It was a retrogressive holdover from pre–Civil War days in the South, a rock-ribbed bastion of conservatism and segregation. Our plant was aging and old-fashioned. Its employees were mostly black, and it was organized by the UAW. The rates of alcoholism, suicide, and drug addiction in the town were among the highest in the country. I sometimes volunteered the ironic thought that if Charles Dickens had visited us in Bolivar, he would have felt he had never left the grimier parts of London.

There, in 1970, I learned an unforgettable lesson. One day at the plant, during the second shift, the buzzer signaling the long-standing 10:00 P.M. ten-minute coffee break failed. Management determined that since it knew how to activate another buzzer, it would reschedule the coffee break for ten minutes later, at ten minutes after 10:00. It was at that point that an uneducated, elderly black man (any black man in his fifties or older was elderly in Bolivar) with the wonderfully biblical name of Nobi Cross changed my life.

Nobi worked in the polish-and-buff department. It was a terrible place to work. The twelve operators there were required to hold zinc castings against a buffing wheel to polish the castings. The process sprayed the buffing compound into the air and into the operators' lungs. Those who worked in that department eagerly anticipated the coffee break.

When he learned that the break was to be rescheduled, Nobi Cross stopped buffing and spoke up. "I don't work for no buzzer," he said. "The buzzer works for me." In his own way, Nobi was declaring that the purpose of technology is to serve the user—not to intimidate or control him. He understood that the only purpose of the buzzer was to announce when it was 10:00 P.M. Since he had a watch, he needed no further assistance. And so when it was ten o'clock, Nobi Cross, followed by his co-workers, walked to his coffee break.

All hell broke loose at the plant. Workers don't take it upon themselves to determine when they take a break. The managers quickly suspended everybody involved. Sitting comfortably removed in my office at Harman International on Long Island, I received news of the eruption. I called Dr. Michael Maccoby, who had been my doctoral adviser and friend, and together we called Irving Bluestone, who headed the General Motors division of the United Auto Workers. The three of us decided to fly to Bolivar to straighten things out. It would set a critical course for me.

As we talked to the workers about what they did and how they felt, we received an education on what their work lives were like. Michael was told by one worker on an assembly line, "I do this two thousand times a day," referring to the task that was his job. Maccoby asked him, "What do you think about?" He replied: "I think about nothing. I just watch the yellow line running down the center of the assembly line."

Well, try putting a cemented surround onto a small automobile speaker thirty times a minute, eighteen hundred times an hour, eight hours a day. Or try spending your days in a polish-and-buff department, feeding small die castings onto fixtures revolving at a set rate while a thin film of dirt and dust clogs the air, clogs your throat, and clogs your mind. For the first time I could feel what it was like to yield any sense of individuality and freedom the moment an employee appeared at work. I could see him inhibited by the very nature of what he was doing, from sharing a moment with a neighbor or experiencing any sense of craftsmanship. I could understand the hate for the foreman, who was trapped in the same madness as he pressed the employees for more and better when they had come to believe that more meant worse.

I imagined myself getting out of bed in the morning, looking forward only to returning in the evening with no wish to do anything but grab a beer and sit numbly before the television. What must it be like, I wondered, to be convinced that what you're doing now you'll do the rest of your life? To sense your own worthlessness? That was how it was to be an assembly line worker in our factory in Bolivar.

I realized then that the way I ran the plant in Bolivar and at other Harman factories was in contradiction to everything I was doing at Friends World College. The potential parallels were obvious. Our workers were like the college's students; the supervisors could fulfill the role of the faculty. If a progressive view of education could lead to the leaps of imagination and learning I was seeing at FWC, shouldn't the same principles be equally productive in a factory? Was it unreasonable to expect that if the workers were given enlarged responsibility, their response would be constructive? Would the supervisors, freed from the roles of warden and sheriff and reestablished as knowledgeable resources, flourish? I was determined at that moment to attempt it. Our attempt became known as the "Bolivar experiment," and it did indeed flourish.

This is what happened in Bolivar. We started a school on the premises during work hours, paid for by the company. That was not so unusual, but this school was different. The emphasis was not on improving skills, or on teaching old workers new tricks. Instead, our school taught what some people within the company knew about and could teach, and what some employees wanted to learn. There were classes in English and fundamental mathematics, classes in health and music.

We had an old upright piano on the premises. Twelve students learned to play by first constructing cardboard keyboards on which they learned the fingering, and then transferred it to the real piano. The combination of studying things they wanted to learn and teaching things they wanted to share generated a culture of personal development that led to growing self-esteem, mutual respect, and regard for the company.

Nowhere was the effort more focused than on the supervisors and other middle managers in the company. It has been commonplace, during efforts to overhaul or reengineer companies, to concentrate on the top and the bottom of the organizational pyramid. Everything in my experience tells me that you overlook the middle managers at your peril. They are the ones who, more than the senior executives, make the trains run. They are the ones who can most easily disrupt or inhibit change because they are the ones who are most naturally challenged by it. The familiar expression is, "I came up the hard way with a supervisor's foot on my neck. Now that I have finally emerged from the pack, no one is going to dilute my power, remove a single one of my perks, or violate my sovereignty." Persuading the middle manager that there is more to gain, more to learn, and more to contribute in this new arrangement is key. Persuading the middle managers is also the best way to move through the organization to the next level. It does not come easy, but when it works, the total plan is facilitated and great things can happen.

I saw no better expression of that than the creation of the *Bolivar Mirror*, the company newspaper. It was a newspaper totally unlike those produced in our other company facilities around the country. The others were altogether typical of the genre. Printed on glossy paper, they were dominated by a message from the president and puffed with information about social events, baseball scores, etc. By contrast, the *Bolivar Mirror* encouraged the employees to write about their families, their feelings, and their aspirations. Stories of the old country, remembrances of mama, and articles critical of management dominated its pages. It was more widely read in our other divisions than were the divisions' own papers.

I remember the first time I went back to Bolivar after the newspaper was initiated. We had a large multipurpose meeting room, and submissions for the first issue were spread across a big oak table. The editor asked when I would have time to review and select among the pieces. She expected me to be the censor. I clarified that in a hurry. Neither I nor anyone in senior management would play that role. The editor was to select the offerings based on quality and diversity. The only qualification was that obscenity and ad hominem attacks would not be permitted. Word spread quickly; it led to a vibrant newspaper which, among its other attractions, included several attacks on management and on CEO Sidney Harman himself. I was free to respond in the next issue. And I did.

The *Bolivar Mirror* was an important part of a new foundation. Supervisors were encouraged to share their knowledge and their responsibilities with the line workers. One day I asked Paul, who supervised line 1, whether he had any fear about yielding so much power to the people he supervised. His reply captures the first of my lessons: "I notice that the more power I give, the more power I get." That was the essence of the Bolivar experiment—a program widely recognized as the first effort in American industrial history to alter the traditional adversarial relationship between workers and managers.

I was often asked whether our practice of authorizing the production line workers to halt the line if quality fell was tantamount to turning the place over to the employees. "Aren't you telling the children to just go play in the sandbox?" I was asked. Over time, the answer became very clear. As trust in management grew and as responsibility was delegated to the production workers, their self-respect grew, they assumed more responsibility, and the plant became more productive. Alcoholism, suicide, and drug addiction in the Bolivar plant virtually disappeared. In a town where employees had been harassed and oppressed, some of those reenergized employees ran for election to the

Board of Education, others for political office. As the plant was transformed, the families and the community were transformed.

My friend and right hand at the time, Sandy Berlin, was so passionate about the program that he literally moved to Bolivar so he could live and work there as we proceeded with our experiment. Sandy's contribution to the experiment and his support of my efforts were invaluable. He left the company a few years later to pursue his interest in real estate, and he did very well. Eventually he would purchase a small, elite, top-end high-fidelity electronics maker—the Mark Levinson Company. Later still, he would sell it to us.

The Bolivar experience has shaped my approach to business for more than thirty years. I have applied its principles everywhere, and although results have varied and that sense of youthful, romantic enthusiasm has been difficult to replicate, the practices have led consistently to higher productivity and widespread respect for those who do the work.

Nobi Cross's indelible remark—"The buzzer works for me"—reminds me again and again that technology must be subordinate to the people it serves. In the factory it is the people who make a company thrive or stumble. Honoring them, recognizing their effort, inspiring them to release their know-how, and making new technology their servant pays off.

American industry has been in thrall to the notion that the cost of a product will be enormously reduced if you either produce the product offshore in low-labor-rate nations, or, better yet, outsource the manufacturing to such places. In the electronics industry it was commonplace only a few years ago that direct labor cost constituted as much as 15 percent of material, labor, and overhead. At the time, offshore manufacturing might have been seductive if there were not other considerations. For me, the most important of those considerations is the reality that many creative product leaps occur on the factory floor, and a significant percentage of those come from the people in the direct labor force. Today, for a combination of technological and manufacturing reasons, direct labor represents somewhat less than 5 percent of material, labor, and overhead in our company, and it is headed lower. How much of a genius does it take to recognize that when it falls below 1 percent, it does not matter whether the manufacturing is done in Indiana or in Indonesia? Further, when you manufacture offshore in low-labor-rate countries, there are additional unpredictable but often-significant costs that arise from problems in the offshore facility. When a crisis of quality or product failure develops, the need to dispatch the best talent from the homeland is unavoidable. The cost and disruptions that triggers at home cannot be ignored.

And once you yield the manufacturing to others, you become dependent on them. I much prefer to roll my own. I am certain that in the midterm and the long term, it generates extra benefits for the company.

Our respect for manufacturing and diversity has produced some unusual results. In highly conservative Martinsville, Indiana, the center of our OEM manufacturing—a stunning breakthrough. Andrea Burls-Derrer is young, African-American, and female—and she heads all manufacturing there. Her appointment was not my doing, but it was surely the result of my commitment, writ large—a genuine full-opportunity employer. Martinsville is fundamentally a manufacturing operation. The engineering and marketing for this important component of our OEM business is now conducted at the engineering center in Farmington Hills, in the Detroit suburbs. Engineers and manufacturing people from Farmington Hills are frequently in Martinsville, and manufacturing people from Martinsville are frequently at Farmington Hills—no colonies there. But Andrea is the most senior person resident in the Martinsville plant. Everyone there loves her because, quite simply, she knows what she is doing and because our people welcome her professionalism.

In our factories in California and Germany, old-style assembly lines have yielded to software-driven, software-controlled lines. In the old method, each assembly line would be staffed with workers sitting shoulder to shoulder and facing their counterparts across the line. Each person would contribute another element in the growing assembly, and every few yards along the line, a calibration of the product or an interim test would be conducted. Defective products would be removed from the line to be repaired and later reintroduced. Ultimately the product would reach final inspection and test.

On our new software-processed production lines there are many fewer operators because the products are designed to test and calibrate themselves, and for some operations they are, quite remarkably, designed to repair themselves as the line moves. That progress in line and manufacturing design has also had positive consequences for the workers. They have learned new, upgraded skills. They now can service the instrumentation that controls the production lines. There are fewer of them for the same volume of business because the lines do much of the work themselves. And as those new production lines become more efficient and more productive, our products become less costly to manufacture, the sales volume grows, and the number of employees remains essentially steady. Each produces more product value every day.

In the past, large old-line companies could take refuge in the knowledge that scale separated and protected them from small, aspiring firms. The big boys had the capital required to set up and run as many lines as they needed, and they had the capital to tear them down and tool up others. Today our software-processed manufacturing lines are key to our digital factories. It is relatively easy for us to set up one or a number of them. We can enlarge or duplicate our factories quickly and relatively inexpensively to accommodate large increases in demand. We are in a new age in which this new reality makes us as big as competitors with five and ten times our sales volume.

We look to our people as central, and they look to us for reciprocity. You might think of it as a new social contract—a "more for more" arrangement in which each side contributes more and each side gets more in return.

It was not always so for me. I grew up at Bogen with the traditional attitudes about management. Everything was top down, and the people who did the work were essentially replaceable parts in the machinery. The teachings of Frederick Taylor and scientific management were dominant. The mantra was

"Reduce the work to the simplest common denominator—the best worker is a dumb person unburdened by thought." Nobi Cross altered my thinking forever. He stimulated many of our programs and gave focus to our principles.

I am convinced that those principles are equally applicable to service businesses. My friend David Hellman is chairman of the Department of Medicine at Johns Hopkins University, and he is the physician-in-chief of the Johns Hopkins Bayview Medical Center. His is the top executive position in a large, prestigious medical facility. David is one of the century's leading medical minds on vasculitis, and he has done superb research in the area. I was therefore very surprised when, in July 2000, he took his position as a high-level manager. He visited me when I was an overnight patient at the hospital, and we talked about his new experience—how the janitors had protested, not over wages, but over disrespect and a loss of dignity. One had said, "When I am cleaning the floor and come to a place where two doctors are standing talking, they do not move. I must clean around them. They don't even know I'm there, and if they do, they don't think that I am worth moving for." Dr. Hellman spent time that morning at an assembly with the doctors of the hospital talking about dignity. "When we reviewed a new procedure, the doctors all spoke with enthusiasm about how they had planned it. But when I asked whether they had talked with any patients, they were downright puzzled," he told me. I said to him, "Do you realize that we have exactly the same problems? You should write your own book."

Valuing Your Employees

Years ago, on Thanksgiving Day in 1957, our lone factory in Westbury, New York, burned to the ground. It broke my heart— we had everything tied up in that place and all of it had vanished. When the smoke cleared, I determined to rebuild and restore it as it had been. That is what we did, and in due course the fire was a memory. But in truth we had learned very little from the sad experience. Then in 1994 our largest domestic factory, in Northridge, California, was struck by a horrific earthquake. We were at its epicenter.

In 1957 the Westbury plant had been 50,000 square feet and employed 200 people. In 1994 the Northridge plant, at more than 500,000 square feet, was ten times as big and employed 1,500 workers. The earthquake destroyed all of the nearby roads and virtually demolished our entire facility. But our people had come to care about the company; it was much more than just a job. They came every day to help the contractors rebuild, although for many the trip took as long as eight hours because of the destruction all around us. In only ten days we were back in operation.

It took four months to fully recover, but we did not simply rebuild it as it was. We took advantage of the opportunity to listen when the workers told us about more effective ways to feed and control the lines. We listened, and we applied what we learned. Our people showed that caring for them over the years had triggered a stunning response when a crisis hit us. Most plants in the area were out of business for over a year.

One of the early programs we created in the Northridge plant was called "Ole"—off-line enterprises. When market conditions drove a decline in demand for our products, we moved people from the traditional production lines to the off-line enterprises. There, we would unashamedly create work for the temporarily unneeded workers. For example, each day we cut thousands of circles of wood, 8, 10, and 12 inches in diameter, from the front of loudspeaker cabinets to permit the loudspeaker cones to access the air. For many years the circles had been discarded as scrap. For Ole we purchased small, inexpensive clock movements and mounted them on the wooden circles, which had been polished and finished in glossy colors. The new wall-hanging clocks that resulted were used as marketing tools and gifts to hospitals and other charities. And they found modest markets in hardware stores.

We brought back work that had been contracted to cable and harness makers, and we searched for other ways, such as maintenance and security, to keep the displaced workers employed even as we sought to generate healthier markets. Yes, it cost money, but it was offset by the hidden costs associated with reductions in force and the ultimate rehiring of people—costs we would now avoid. Most important, a message was sent to our people about where the company's heart lay. That was not lost on our workforce.

In plants across the country we established one of our more rewarding programs, the Senior Executive Service. It was, and continues to be, a novel and valuable idea. SES requires the senior executives of the company to set aside a minimum number of days each year to work on active production lines in our facto- ries. The activity connects the executives to regular production people—contacts that would otherwise rarely occur. The execu- tives learn a great deal about what it takes to produce a quality product, and the production people learn that the executives are human, reasonable, and often clumsily incompetent as they at- tempt to do factory jobs. The experience generates a sense of mutual goodwill and adds to the conviction among our employ- ees that this is a company they want to work for. I participate, too, and it is always a great experience.

In another plant, where the workforce is organized and repre- sented by a labor union, we had tripped over our good inten- tions. A five-year contract was coming to its end, and our expectation was that it would be renewed with an attractive in- crease in hourly wages. Local management was confident that an agreement would be reached quickly. They were wrong. The union voted the agreement down by an astonishing four-to-one margin. The defeat led to a serious awakening, and to my per- sonal intervention. When I visited with them, the employees made clear that they welcomed the increased wages but were alienated by what they saw as management's disrespect and by a loss of dignity in their lives. A series of intense and candid meet- ings produced new, mutual pledges. That might have seemed enough, but with the union's cooperation we took it a step fur- ther. A novel new committee, entitled the "How We Doin'?" Committee, was formed to continually monitor whether the personal, emotional, and human aspects of the agreement were being respected. The committee does its job, the plant flourishes, and the spirit of the meetings is honored.

We had earlier created a program called Cost Saving Sharing. I was convinced that traditional profit-sharing plans were seriously flawed. They were usually initiated at times of full employment when management was seeking ways to keep people from leaving for more attractive opportunities. Stimulated by that environment, the profit-sharing plans were seductive and employees bought in. The same vigorous economic environment pretty well guaranteed that there would be profits to share. Employers welcomed the plans and managers felt good about them, but few employees understood the real meaning of profits to be shared or recognized that in business, one might also experience losses. Management rarely found the time to offer the kind of guidance that provided the basis for such understanding. It rarely marketed the program to the employees. The result was that over the years, employees participating in such plans would come to see profit sharing as an entitlement. When the inevitable period of decline or loss occurred, the employees did not have a clue and felt ill treated and very disappointed. That is hardly a prescription for creating goodwill in a firm. That kind of experience was distressing and frustrating enough when the economy was healthy, but in a poor economy or when poor business decisions were made by management, employees who had done their part saw themselves as victims.

The central idea in Harman's cost-saving/sharing plan was that excellent work by the production line employee would earn extra rewards, independent of what managers or others might do. It empowered the individual to make a positive contribution that would be recognized. Standards were set for the cost of each operation and each production line. When those standards were beaten, the improvement could be readily expressed in dollars. The improvement—the savings—was shared by the individual employee and the company. Over the years our cost-saving/sharing plan has stimulated many cost improvement proposals from employees, and the standards have frequently been exceeded. These days the sharing can amount to a bonus equal to 10 percent or more of wages—a serious reward. The plan is equally effective in good times or poor. In difficult times it tends to reduce the losses; in good times the company and the employee both earn extra benefits.

Nobi Cross reinforced my instinct that formal education is great, but it's no guarantor of perspective or of respect for diversity and humanity. Those critical elements of leadership can very well arise from empathetic engagement with employees at every level. The dignity, value, and opportunity for personal growth by employees can fuel the development of a company over a lengthy time. When those elements are real—not just public relations pap, it is also very good business.

CHAPTER 5

HIGH FINANCE: SEPARATING THE WHEAT FROM THE CHAFF

In ancient China, the bureaucrats separated
the wheat from the chaff.
They then carefully cataloged the chaff
And discarded the wheat.
—SOURCE: UNKNOWN

I was first persuaded that I had the instincts of an entrepreneur at the end of our first year in business. In that year we produced the original Harman/Kardon tuner and the first Harman/Kardon amplifier.

As the year ended, I found myself with an inventory of a hundred pieces of the A100 amplifier, our original product—even as its successor model was starting into production. Eager to cleanse the old inventory, I authorized our sales representative in

California to offer the entire quantity to Radio Television Supply Corporation, then Los Angeles' largest distributor. That offer, I understood, needed to be a bargain. I suggested that we reduce the price; the salesman should offer the lot to Radio Television Supply's owner, Sol Shuper, for eighty dollars each.

This was 1953, a half century ago, and for us it was a very big deal. Indeed, I authorized the salesman to telephone me collect from Mr. Shuper's office. When he did, I heard Mr. Shuper's practiced voice, patronizing me.

"How are you, kid?"

"I'm fine, Mr. Shuper."

"Good, kid. I understand that you want to unload those hundred amplifiers. A good move. Send them along and I'll put my check for seven thousand dollars in the mail tonight."

"Oh, Mr. Shuper. There seems to be a misunderstanding," I gasped. "The price is eighty dollars. That means a check for eight thousand," I squeaked.

"You a gambling man, son?"

"The scourge of Las Vegas, Mr. Shuper."

"I'll toss you for it."

Gulp. A thousand dollars was a lot of money back then. "You're on," I said.

"Good," said Mr. Shuper. "Toss. I'll call."

I managed a hoarse, "No. You toss. I'll call."

That was the moment! My immediate instinct was to anticipate how the next steps would develop—I had arrived as an entrepreneur.

A moment's hesitation, and then from Mr. Shuper, "Okay. I've tossed. What's your call?"

"Tails," I said.

There was a terrifying pause at the other end of the line. Finally, an annoyed voice, "Okay. Ship the damn things. I'll send you eight thousand dollars tonight."

Twelve months later I encountered Sol Shuper at the Hilton Hotel in Chicago. "You SOB," he said to me. "I tossed heads. But I was sure that if I said so, you would think I was cheating a poor kid. You got me!"

It was a lesson I have never forgotten. It would serve me well thereafter. In the fall of 1986, six years after reacquiring Harman International from Beatrice and operating it as a highly leveraged, privately owned company, we determined to go public. I found myself sitting in an impressive meeting room at the prestigious investment firm, Goldman Sachs.

Goldman was then, as it is now, widely regarded as one of the premier banking firms in the world, and we were about to launch an initial public offering. I represented Harman International, and Robert Rubin, who would eventually become a legendary secretary of the treasury under President Clinton, was the Goldman lead. There were twenty Goldman people in the room and at least one hundred more on the conference call as we hammered out the offering price and the spread. Spread, you'll remember, is the term used to identify the commission percentage earned by the bank. We managed to agree on the offering price but disagreed on the rate. Goldman proposed 6 per-

97

cent and Harman proposed 4 percent. After considerable argument, I summoned that earlier experience and suggested to Bob Rubin, "It's late, and we've been arguing this a long time. What do you say we toss for it?"

He quickly responded, "You're on."

When I said, "Great. You toss, I'll call," he reacted: "I'm the senior figure here. You toss, I'll call." I tossed. He called. He lost. We did the deal at 4 percent.

High finance as it is practiced in the real world is frequently a great deal simpler, less complicated, less sophisticated, and less mysterious than it is usually presented. But much of high finance depends on that very aura of sophistication and inside knowledge. It is a good thing to recognize that nearly all of it reduces to pretty straightforward common sense. And it is a very good thing not to be intimidated and not to hesitate to ask. "Please explain the process to me. I know very well how to make the product we sell, but yours is another world, and I need some help understanding it." That may seem an invitation to more, not less, artfulness, but I have found that by insisting on simple explanations, the mystery disappears and with it most of the nonsense.

Years later we were doing a secondary offering through Montgomery Securities. Bernie Girod, then my chief financial officer– now our CEO—and I were completing the necessary but always exhausting road trip during which we presented our offering to bankers and other investor groups across the country. Weary and eager to see it end, I recognized that once again we had permitted the decision on the spread to wait until the last moment. With some irritation, I spoke to John Berg, the young investment banker traveling with us. "I told your boss weeks ago that I wanted to have the matter of the spread settled long before the final night, and here we are again, three miles up in the air, and it's unsettled. I'm annoyed!"

Remembering my story of our IPO with Goldman Sachs, John replied, "Will you toss for it?"

I asked, in some astonishment, "Are you authorized to do this?"

"God, I hope so. Toss," said John. "I'll call."

"The hell you will," I replied. "I'm the senior person here. You toss. We'll call."

John agreed. He tossed. I asked Bernie to call. Bernie called tails; it was heads. It is not a given, of course, that luck or providence will go your way. I took our loss with total equanimity. "Bernie," I suggested, "get out of the plane." The culprit stayed, of course, and the financing moved swiftly and smoothly to its conclusion.

Balance Sheet Fundamentals

There is nothing fancy or complicated about financial fundamentals. A company must be profitable. That may seem obvious, but it is astonishing how often it does not seem to be a priority. Certainly, if one is following the unconventional management practices and emphases that I promote, the company, especially a public company, had better be profitable. No one wants to hear that "honoring employees" is critical if the business leader expounding that view is also explaining why the company is filing for Chapter 11.

A solid financial base is fundamental. Debt should not exceed equity. A debt to equity ratio of 1 to 1 or better should be the goal, so that a company's leader and key executives do not spend all their time paying bills, meeting the payroll, and keeping the banks happy. In new companies that doesn't come easily, but it should be any company's primary objective. Then top management can have the time to pay attention to the creative building of the firm.

I did not leave the Bogen Company as one committed to a strong balance sheet, though I might well have been. Mr. Bogen's whole approach was just that, although it was essentially intuitive and never articulated. When I did the leveraged repurchase of Harman International in 1980, I borrowed heavily, and our debt to equity ratio was skewed toward the side of debt. But I listened to the good counsel of noted financier Ala Patricof, who urged me to work down the debt as soon a could. "The easy days will come to an end, and those investment-grade balance sheets will have a major leg up." was very valuable guidance. My responsiveness to thei was fully matched by our other executives and by ou d. Today, at a time when so many onetime high flyers have collapsed or fallen precariously, our strong balance sheet is a platform for continued progress.

We have a regular process for annual business planning and budgeting—a procedure everyone understands and anticipates.

That procedure builds a reliable foundation for the business. Budgeting should not be a sterile process. The plan should not be created and then ignored. It is crucial that it be a living instrument, a contract among the leaders, and the reference against which monthly performance is measured and evaluated.

At Harman we review each month four separate times. First we develop the annual budget, expressed as twelve fully detailed months. Then each unit manager is required to prepare a detailed end of the month (EOM) statement projecting how the month will end and comparing it with the original budget. The EOM is required by the 25th of each month. With only a week to go, a good manager should have a very good grasp of how the month is shaping up. If he doesn't, something is wrong. At the same time, a beginning of the month (BOM) forecast is made. It offers the manager's best sense of the next month, which begins in a week. Finally, there is the actual performance for the month as reported by the accounting department. Thus for each month we have a budget, a BOM forecast, an EOM appraisal, and the final actual. It may seem like a lot of budgeting, but the procedure provokes disciplined review and analysis at a time when variances can be identified and creative action can still be taken.

PROFIT AND LOSS FUNDAMENTALS

As awareness of malfeasance at some public companies has grown, a number of companies whose performance has seemed too smooth to be true have come under scrutiny. Is the steady reporting of corporate profits quarter-by-quarter real, or is it the result of "managing the profits"? "How can it be that quarter after quarter, this outfit reports earnings just a penny or two better than Wall Street has forecast?" the doubters ask. The question suggests that the regularity of the profit reports may result from playing with reserves and otherwise manipulating the numbers to produce the appearance of steady progress. Although such practices are less nefarious than the creation of fictitious sales and earnings, they do present a distorted picture of performance—and are, therefore, wrong.

We do not manage profits. We manage expectations, the expectations of the investment community and security analysts who regularly follow Harman International and who provide research to their clients. We do our best to keep them informed of our progress and of our stumbles, if we stumble. It is our job to make sure, consistent with legal requirements, that the investment community can predict with some accuracy how the reporting period will look. If we are on top of our business, if our EOM/BOM practice is effective, we know, and through us our stockholders and the analysts know. There is little surprise then when our actual numbers correspond to their consensus. They and their clients have been well informed. There is a large difference between managing the profits and managing the expectations.

One thing that puzzles me is the analysts' reaction when companies announce detailed plans of restructuring. They tend to ignore the so-called onetime restructuring charges when the company's performance is reviewed. Those charges are, in effect, set aside as somehow irrelevant to the real and measured operating performance. They seem to be viewed as a free ride and an opportunity to clean up the operating statement and the balance sheet without penalty. Some companies seem to generate onetime restructurings every year. Perhaps the financial community believes that when a company does a thorough restructuring, it has rid itself of the unproductive assets that previously depressed its earnings. The company should therefore have an improved earnings outlook. Still, a series of restructurings should cause one to ponder the true earnings of such a company. Observing them, the investment community may conclude that excess reserves are being salted away to decorate the earnings reports of later periods.

The chairman or the CEO need not be a financial or accounting expert, but he should be financially literate. Indeed, there is something to be said for the top manager who understands the material but is not an expert. It is the very seeking of understanding and the requirement that it be expressed in simple and unambiguous language that can assure a minimum of heavy-handedness and a maximum of light.

The numbers are merely symbols for the important stuff. What counts is knowing what those numbers really mean. I buy into nothing I do not understand, and the more convoluted or sophisticated the material, the more determined I am to understand it. I have never forgotten my experience in government, being "snowed" by some who knew the jargon and used it to obscure rather than clarify. As a result, I always reject the suggestion that "this is too complex for you to understand." I prefer the

Warren Buffett view. "If I don't understand it, I'll invest the time and energy to get that understanding. If you can't teach and persuade me, I'll pass on it."

In Harman International's annual report for the fiscal year 2002, the fourth member of our jazz quartet, our chief financial officer, Frank Meredith, wrote the following. I include it here because it shows how challenging it can be to do what is right, and because it shows one way to do it.

Earlier essays have spoken of our business philosophy. I will comment on how it affects our financial and tax planning. We, like most good-sized companies, frequently receive sophisticated proposals for the reduction of taxes. This is an area we pay a great deal of attention to, especially because a high percentage of our total profits is generated in Europe.

Among the proposals we received recently was one that recommended the transfer of a portfolio of intangible assets to a low-tax-rate country such as the Cayman Islands. We were advised that by doing so we could significantly reduce our European taxes. We reviewed the proposal thoroughly and rejected it because we found it weak in theory and unworkable in the structure of our business. It might work in another company, differently organized from our own—one, for example, with a central engineering department. We would have been obliged to create a structure merely for the purpose of this financial engineering. We chose not to.

In recent years, we acquired several European software companies to increase our engineering capacity in that critical area and to accommodate the significant automotive OEM business already committed to us. When the acquisitions were completed, we reorganized our European corporate structure to enhance our ability to deal effectively with labor laws, capital requirements, benefit structures, and corporate governance. As part of that process, we were also able to take advantage of opportunities under current European tax laws to improve the tax efficiency of our European operations. Tax laws and regulations vary widely from country to country, and they often change—as frequently as every year. There is no permanent set of tax laws or regulations.

Our responsibility to our shareholders is to generate world-class products and to earn appropriate profits on their sale. Where do we draw the line when we work at effective financial management? Our guiding principle is that it must comply with the relevant legislation in each country where we do business and are taxed, and it must be consistent with rational, logical, and orderly business practice.

We saw the plan we rejected as a questionable piece of financial engineering. We saw the one we accepted as the natural derivative of a structural change that provided a serious and legitimate tax opportunity, an opportunity vigorously promoted by the European nation.

I present the contrast of the two examples because, though we are prudent, we are also vigilant. We receive new proposals virtually every month, and we reject virtually all of them as excessive because they do not meet our strict standards.

Frank's essay deals with how we balance shareholder interest with the honorable conduct of the business. A leader cannot know every sophisticated device, nor can he be expected to understand the intricacies of every law, regulation, and rule prom-

105

ulgated by Congress and the oversight agencies. But he or she can and must set the operating standard and create the ethical base. It is not enough to say, "I want to be honest" or "I want to pass examination." There is always large room for the exercise of judgment, for determining whether a matter is financially material or financially valid. That judgment he must be able to make.

And the law is not immutable. Today's permissible action, today's good practice, may have been illegal or in violation of the regulations just a year or ten years ago. The rules for GAAP (generally accepted accounting principles) change, and it is therefore critical that a senior manager stay abreast of those changes. As an example, consider goodwill (the amount paid in excess of identified value). For many years the financial accounting standard required that goodwill be amortized over the life of the acquired asset. That would often result in a substantial charge to profits each year. The new financial accounting standard requires that the asset not be amortized but rather tested each year to determine whether its value continues. If it does continue, no charge is to be made. As a result, reported profits in the very same circumstances would be reported as substantially higher.

CAPITAL EXPENDITURES

Capital expenditures and working capital are important in any business; they are especially so in manufacturing companies because they represent the bulk of the firm's cash outlay and must therefore be closely monitored.

Working capital can be converted into cash relatively quickly because it consists principally of accounts receivable, inventory, and accounts payable. If inventories are growing too large, management can reduce that investment through sale and conversion of the excess into cash.

Capital investment on the other hand consists primarily of money used for land, buildings, machinery, and equipment. Those things are not fungible and cannot be converted into cash easily. Errors in inventory can be costly, but they can be dealt with in fairly short order. Errors in capital spending can be much more costly and invariably take far longer to correct. Investments in land and buildings should be undertaken with special caution because they typically carry a heavy price tag and are almost always impossible to sell without heavy penalty. New facilities can be particularly dangerous because they represent substantial new overhead and because once the space has been acquired, organizations have a way of filling it up whether they need it or not. Today, efficient manufacturing techniques and efficient space planning can lead to more production using less space, with a corresponding reduction in new bricks and mortar required.

In well-controlled organizations, the control of capital expenditures follows a familiar pattern. First, a capital budget is prepared as part of the next year's business plan. The budget is reviewed by corporate managers who must determine whether the funds will be invested in the proper sectors of the business and whether the projects make financial sense. Approval of an overall budget should never grant anyone the right to go spend the money. That authorization should be rendered on a project-by-project basis—each project submitted for approval separately. This is where well-intended action can turn to mischief. As justification for the project is developed, the required capital investment is stated, the relevant financial statements are prepared, and the return on investment (ROI) and payback are calculated. In most companies, ROI thresholds are established. Meet or exceed that threshold, or the project is disapproved. When numbers of projects are vying for approval, it is usual practice to rank them in terms of ROI and, in the absence of a more compelling argument, the project with the most attractive apparent ROI is approved.

Unfortunately, despite the fact that the financial statements presenting the ROI often leave the impression of a very precise process with returns calculated to decimal points, the process of evaluating a project cannot be precise. It is of necessity based on a series of assumptions and outright guesses. For example, a capital request to invest in a new production line to build a new product must include assumptions about the pricing of the product, its burdened cost, its annual volume, and its useful life. The more optimistic the assumptions, the higher the calculated returns. Whether the cost estimates are valid, what the useful life of the product is, and whether the market responds well can be determined only in real time. The financial exercise required to prepare a capital spending request is nonetheless a useful one, for it can reveal the critical variables. The opportunity for abuse in order to obtain approval for one's pet project is there, however, and must be recognized.

Because the base against which proposed new capital projects are measured is seldom questioned and easily misunderstood, the opportunity for mischief is enhanced. Investment in the new product is often weighed against investment in a current product nearing the end of its useful life. That calculation can be highly misleading. Many investments in expensive new computer systems have led to great disappointment because the rationale was based on the proclaimed limitations of the predecessor system. The most seductive of the presentations is the one that demonstrates the greatest ROI. It had better be clearly justified before it is approved.

Some argue that a postcompletion audit and review will keep management honest because it requires the reporting of actual results compared with the original assumptions. Unfortunately, conditions frequently change so substantially as to make the process nearly worthless. Investments often become commingled, major changes are frequently made to new products—it becomes nearly impossible to generate a clean, useful postcompletion review. A substantial and statistically significant number of such reviews would be required to provide a useful assessment of management's capital investment performance.

What then is the best way to manage capital expenditures? It is, after all, serious stuff. If he does nothing else, a conscientious leader makes certain that the budget is one the company can live with. This person makes certain that the capital dollars to be spent are used in sectors where they are most likely to produce a good return—sectors showing historically good growth and profitability or those in which a strategic justification can be truly developed. In the end, as individual projects are reviewed, the good leader must go with a gut feeling. Does the project make sense? Is it something, given the hazards, he is prepared to put himself on the line for? In the end, that exercise of critical judgment is what management is all about.

BUYING BACK STOCK

Repurchasing a company's own stock is one of those areas demanding critical judgment. Any instinct to buy your own company's stock in an effort to prevent its price from declining, or in an effort to drive it up, is not only illegal, it is feckless. It just won't work. The best reason to employ the company's cash to buy in its own stock is the judgment that the purchase represents the best investment the company can make. After all, the CEO knows more about the company, about its prospects, and about its stock price, than about any other company or any other investment for which the company might use its funds. At Harman International we have conditioned that judgment with the determination that any repurchase of our own stock must add to earnings (in accounting jargon, it must be P&L accretive). The ownership of those shares, adjusted to the cost of the money used to purchase them, must result in an increase in earnings per share across the outstanding shares. In addition, the use of cash

110

on hand or the borrowing of the cash to effect the purchase must not cause the debt-to-equity ratio to rise above the company's target. If the funds are available, if the balance sheet is not compromised, and if there is no demonstrably better way to use the cash, the decision to buy in one's own stock becomes very simple. I believe that it is the only basis on which it should be done.

P/E MULTIPLES

Companies and investors often make the buy-or-not-buy decision based on a review of the multiple of earnings at which the stock is being traded. Somehow those multiples have taken on outsized meaning. Many otherwise sophisticated investors make decisions on which companies to invest in principally as a function of their trading multiples. I find it a strange phenomenon. It arises out of the sense that multiples are somehow figures of merit determined by the multiple gods or the multiple sheriffs. I have heard otherwise perfectly sensible businesspeople ask, "What's your multiple?" Much as one might ask, "What's your Social Security number?" Somehow a mythology has developed that suggests that, at least within a range, depending on the industry sector in which you are engaged, your multiple is essentially assigned. That's nonsense. A multiple does not influence or drive the market price of any stock. It is the other way around. The price is driven only by what analysts recommend and buyers are prepared to pay. Once the price exists, you can calculate the multiple of earnings that it represents. The utility of the multiple is only as a metric, a distillation of how the market, that strange, anthropomorphic beast, currently responds to the company's earnings.

For years we were reluctant to make public declarations that the core of the Harman business was the design and manufacture of electronic systems for the automakers. Such a declaration, we feared, would bracket us with conventional suppliers to the automakers. Historically, those suppliers were regarded as doomed to cyclically low earnings, and those low earnings provoked low stock prices.

Ultimately we swallowed our timidity and presented ourselves boldly to the financial community. We said that the core of our business was automotive OEM, but that it would be a terrible error to catalog us with typical, conventional automotive OEM suppliers. The conventional supplier was seen as a company eager to sell a product or service that the automotive buyer identified as a commodity—a product he could purchase from a dozen or more vendors. That perspective permitted the buyer to arbitrarily establish the specifications, the delivery schedule, and the price. We bore no resemblance to that model. We had become the automakers' engineering department. They depended on us so that they might be relieved of the cost of maintaining their own. They looked to us for world-class manufacturing, and they looked to us for our product brand.

It was that brand (Harman/Kardon, Mark Levinson, JBL, or Infinity) that authenticated their participation in premium music systems—and these days, in elaborated infotainment/telematics systems. More and more auto companies around the world were recognizing the marketing value and profitability available in our systems. More and more of those automakers were applying the systems to more and more car platforms, and the numbers and the percentage of buyers who chose to have them were increasing every year. Furthermore, as the systems became more complex and more elaborate, the typical selling price to the automotive customer multiplied anywhere from four to eight times.

As such, we were not a conventional OEM supplier. Over time, as our argument was repeated and the company prospered, the financial analysts and fund managers began to agree, and valued our stock accordingly. The price rose, and because it did the calculation represented by dividing the market price of the stock by the earnings per share produced a multiple substantially above the typical, cyclical automotive multiple; indeed, above the Standard and Poor's average.

But again, I fuss about the multiple because it should be seen as derivative, and because if it is not seen that way, it can lead to unwise strategic decisions. Many investors make decisions on which companies to invest in almost entirely as a consequence of their trading multiples. Treating the multiple as the expression of the "wisdom" of the market is a lazy substitute for a legitimate attempt to build evaluation based on cash flow and other fundamental business and marketing expressions. I acknowledge that there is some utility in using the multiple as a screening device if you are evaluating a particular company or, more relevantly, if you are attempting arm's length choices among possible investments. But there is no substitute for doing the real work of analyzing a company—speaking to vendors and customers, evaluating the product or technology, and assessing the competence of the management team.

TWO SETS OF BOOKS

The United States government actually authorizes businesses to keep two quite different sets of books—one for reporting the earnings of a public company to its public and another for reporting its taxes to the government. The difference between the two sets of reported numbers reflects a "cash" approach taken by the IRS versus an "accrual" approach taken by the accountants. The IRS does not recognize reserves as expense. While the accountants record a reserve for an uncollectible account as an expense, the IRS will only recognize that expense when the account is written off. Similarly, reserves for obsolete inventory or for warranty expense are not recognized by the IRS as a reduction of earnings. Were they so recognized, they would produce a lower tax. The IRS recognizes those expenses only when they are actually incurred. There are other differences. Assets are depreciated over different periods for book and tax purposes, and the depreciation methods used can be different from each other. The IRS typically allows faster depreciation of assets and certain tax credits such as R&D credits, which is not permitted for book purposes.

The two systems are said to reflect differences in the timing of expenses only and should provide identical results when reviewed over a lengthy period of time. In reality, for most companies there are semipermanent differences between book and tax results. The tax calculations shown on the publicly reported income statement of a company is not the tax the company actually pays. It is, however, the tax that produces the net income figure that appears in the newspapers. That net income figure drives the calculation of earnings per share (EPS) and is a major influence on the price of the company's public stock.

The difference between the two systems adds unnecessary complication without providing meaningful additional information. There is even a third set of books to consider. Many European firms report in accordance with International Accounting Standards. As a consequence, they are required to prepare three sets of books, one according to the International Accounting Standards, another according to U.S. Accounting Standards, and a third according to the tax code in the country of incorporation. I am hopeful that the day will come when publicly reported tax and income numbers will be the same as those reported for tax purposes.

In sum, high finance in business is important all right, but it is often more hype than high. Less mystery and more light, less ambiguity and more directness would make the important work easier—the work of producing excellent products and services that people want to buy.

CHAPTER 6

NEGOTIATING

The brain is a wonderful organ;
it starts working the moment you get up
in the morning
and does not stop until you get into the office.
—ROBERT FROST

During World War II the major consumer electronics companies were engaged exclusively in military manufacturing and feared they would lose their consumer markets. The government had authorized them to spend up to 5 percent of annual revenues on institutional advertising. They were not free to advertise consumer products; in fact, they weren't making any. Capehart did something interesting with its 5 percent. They commissioned paintings on musical themes by such eminent artists as Miro, Chagall, Calder, and Dali. The oils were reproduced in full-page advertisements in *Life* magazine with the signature, *Capehart*

Radio. No doubt, readers of the magazine saw the ads and remembered the name. And the Capehart Company came into possession of a collection of thirteen remarkable paintings.

Then it was that, as a young man, I went to visit the Capehart distributor for the New York area. Daniel Kahn was a pleasant, self-effacing man with a great instinct for the business jugular. I hoped to persuade him to market Harman/Kardon product, but he had no time for that discussion. He was about to drive himself across the George Washington Bridge to New Jersey and the headquarters of mighty IT&T, the conglomerate that had earlier acquired Capehart and which was in the process of selling it to him. "Come along, kid," he suggested. "You will find this interesting."

The two of us walked into a gigantic boardroom, the walls hung with those wonderful paintings, and sitting around the board table an army of executives, lawyers, journalists, and cameramen. Just the two of us and that army. Seated imperially across the table from Kahn was the chairman of IT&T, General Harrison, who had been in charge of all supplies for the American army in World War II.

General Harrison leaned forward expectantly as my host raised his pen to sign the contracts for acquisition. Photographers snapped away; journalists were busy scribbling. Then, with the pen poised in midair, Kahn shook his head and put it down. He repeated the action a moment later, and General Harrison bellowed, "What is the matter?"

"I can't do it," Kahn exhaled.

With the battalion assembled, with his moment of triumph

threatened, the General bellowed again, "And why not?" Kahn, shaking his head sadly, replied, "I must have the paintings." The deal had not included the Capehart paintings. The ceiling, the walls, and the floor shook, but the General could not afford to let the deal fall through. The crisis ended with a delicious compromise: Kahn acquired the company and walked off with half the paintings without cost.

It had been great fun, and it taught me several things I have not forgotten. Over the years, whenever we were wrapping up a deal, I would ask my colleagues, "Where are the paintings?" It has become a prod for finding that something extra that is nearly always available when the other party is so invested in closing the deal that he must yield. The trick, of course, is to ask for just the right something extra—not to overreach.

There was also something about the style of that Capehart meeting, the contrast between this Daniel walking into the lion's den, surrounded by ferocious animals and accompanied by one helpless kid. He had produced a piece of theater that tilted the balance—tilted it incongruously but inescapably toward Daniel. I have used similar theater many times.

The art of negotiating well—and it is an art—is undertaught and underappreciated. There is a subset of business literature on the subject—but at best it reaches only a minority of those who can benefit from it. Much of life involves negotiation—hiring, selling, house buying, personal relationships—and yet it is taken for granted that business managers are prepared and able to negotiate. The intense, extremely complex negotiations in the Middle East involve historical conflicts, cultural differences, personality flaws, and powerful political interests. The issues seem intractable, yet negotiation is the only possible path to resolution.

I have found that negotiating well is a function of experience, preparation, and intuition. All three are requisite to success. It can be great fun because it demands creativity and understanding of the other fellow's needs and instincts while finding the way to the answer you want. While experience and intuition can't be taught, it is possible to look for common threads that apply to all negotiations.

The first is to select the right person on whom to concentrate your attention. This may not be self-evident—it is often not the principal or the lead negotiator. Your target should be the person who, all things considered, is the point of leverage. When Harman was negotiating the purchase of Becker, all the suitors were staying and meeting at the Frankfurt airport hotel in Germany. The whole affair had a Marx Brothers movie quality about it. Every time we left a meeting, it seemed, we would trip over one or another of the challengers as they were coming to or departing their own meetings. A surprisingly large number of participants were involved in the negotiations: buyers, sellers, representatives of the lead bank, and lawyers for everybody in sight.

While the other suitors were all focused on the bank, we found Roland Becker. A cultivated, decent man, although an unsuccessful businessman, he brought enormous personal pride to the situation. He had been the inheritor of a onetime powerful business. His name was still on the door. He cared deeply about

120

who would inherit his company, and he had in fact vetoed a deal the bank had earlier cut with an Asian buyer. Roland was our pivot point, and we concentrated our attention on him. Once he had reached the decision that Harman was the best place for his company, and once he had asserted to his attorney and other counselors that he knew what he was doing, we were free to address the bank. It took a great deal of time to get there, but it took very little time to play our trump card at the bank. They needed Roland's approval and he had given it to us. We had the deal and were gone from Frankfurt while others were still meeting. We had won the negotiation simply by finding the pivotal person— he alone could help us leap the obstacles, whether they were price, currency, timing, style, personality, or compatibility—and bring the matter to closure.

A second critical step is determining what issues are important to you in the negotiation and, critically, what issues are important to them. It is essential to put yourself in their shoes, to figure out exactly what their interests are, and in what order of priority. The primary interest is not always maximizing the price—it may be timing, fit, structure, or prestige. Getting to know the principals on the other side and reviewing their prior performance improves the chances to conclude a deal. It is equally critical to know your own interests—what you must accomplish and where can you give ground. Although every negotiation creates its own rhythm and its own discipline, this kind of preparation is invaluable. It can save a great deal of time, and on occasion it can reveal the judgment that there really is no deal to be done.

My two transactions with Beatrice illustrate this nicely. I was in a difficult position in 1976. I had accepted the Commerce Department position and needed to sell the company quickly— not generally a recipe for a great deal. Yet I was fortunate to encounter a Beatrice Corporation driven by a mindless determination to diversify and acquire. Throughout the early 1970s they had been acquiring businesses as diverse as lamps, shoes, and luggage. Eagerness blinded them to the fact that they did not belong in our business. The price was almost irrelevant. They knew nothing about high fidelity and had no clue how to manage its growing complexity. In retrospect, I realize that I took advantage of their eagerness and gave inadequate attention to what would likely develop afterward. After all, I was committed to government and to saving the nation.

When I repurchased Harman International in 1980, I had a very different Beatrice to measure. They were in trouble and desperate to divest their unwise acquisitions. Recognizing that desperation, realizing that they really had no alternative buyer (although they surely claimed they did) placed me in an advantageous bargaining position, and I used it.

Once you have figured out whom to negotiate with and what you and they are looking for, the fun begins. As I suggested earlier, a negotiation can be as simple as a coin flip or as complex as an algorithm. Laying out the issues in an advantageous way and letting the other party know you are in comfortable command of them can set the negotiation in the right direction. Enthusiasm, properly tempered, can be contagious. The more interested the other fellow is in making the deal happen, the greater the likelihood that it will come your way. I would not, however, recommend the level of enthusiasm expressed by my wife as we were escorted through a house we were thinking of buying in Venice, California. The owner was our guide, and he did it nicely. Jane loved everything she saw and frequently revealed her excitement in his presence. The moment came, however, when she exclaimed, "I love this house; it is seriously underpriced." I knew then that I had a problem. No longer could I negotiate from a position of strength. When it was all over, I congratulated myself because I had persuaded the owner to sell it to us at his asking price.

Taking the other fellow's measure is not child's play, and there is no one sure procedure. Figuring out what will move and excite him is the prime pivot point of the negotiation. Just how eager is he to make the sale or the purchase? How much time, money, pride, or reputation does he have invested? The correct reading can tip the scale.

In virtually every transaction there comes a point of crisis—a moment that tests the mettle of negotiators on both sides—a moment when you must be ready to walk. If you say that you are ready to walk, you better be prepared to walk. If you are bluffing, you can bet you will give it away. You must be unequivocal and you must be ready to accept the consequences. The matter may have nothing to do with value or equity, but it almost certainly has plenty to do with the way the protagonists see themselves. If you are well prepared and strong, it will come across.

The point of the negotiation is not to make the other fellow feel that he has lost, but rather to find a resolution that persuades both parties that they have done well. It is a critical objective, even if you know that you will not deal with the fellow again. A reputation for honest, fair negotiating becomes a strategic advantage in future negotiations. It can be crucial in acquisitions where those with whom you have negotiated will stay with the acquired company.

Many acquired companies have failed because of a silly conceit—that the particulars of a business aren't all that important. "Two pair of pants or two pair of speakers—it doesn't really matter. Good business practice will take care of everything." Well, it won't. Knowing the business, knowing the customers, and knowing those things unique to that operation make a very big difference.

Harman has used acquisitions as a supplement to the organic growth of the company—not as an excuse to build an empire or to shadow the slowing course of a business. On occasion the excesses of another company have provided us with opportunity. The Beatrice fiasco, for example, left the pieces of Harman in a place where the company could be reconstituted fairly quickly and inexpensively. Similarly, Becker became available because its management had squandered its financial and personal resources on a list of business engagements, all of which were foreign to its core. That kind of hubris can kill.

I haven't done the analysis, but I would wager that the majority of acquisitions made during the last ten years of the bull market have failed to deliver any real value to the acquiring company or its shareholders. We have witnessed some spectacular failures—failures where the entire market value of an acquired company disappeared in less than two or three years. Examples abound—AOL Time Warner, Tyco, and WorldCom, to name a few. The heralded synergies sought by the acquiring companies all too seldom materialized. Fundamental cultural conflicts often developed between the two management teams, and the practicalities of integrating two separate organizations frequently resulted in demotivated employees and ineffective operations.

Essentially there are just two kinds of deals: (1) the serious, sober, strategic acquisition that conforms to an existing long-term and explicable plan, and (2) the financial engineering acquisition where the relationship between the price of two public stocks drives the deal.

Harman International has had consistent success in its acquisitions because we have chosen the first—we have sought underlying value and have been guided by key strategic considerations rather than by funny-money arithmetic. Because we have usually acquired companies that were in significant financial difficulty, our cost has been quite modest. Although we have made twenty acquisitions since 1980, acquisition is not the way we have grown. The acquired companies were invariably very small at the time we found them; we built them over the years. For example, when our U.S. automotive OEM company was purchased in 1981, its annual sales were $15 million. Twenty years later its sales exceeded $500 million. We acquired Becker in 1995. Its sales that year were approximately $150 million and it was generating enormous losses. Today Becker sales approach $1 billion, the company is very profitable, and it is growing at almost 50 percent annually. Indeed, the complete automotive

OEM group, of which Becker is a part, now accounts for more than 60 percent of our company's sales. The group was assembled and built through careful attention and serious integration. Accounting systems were rationalized, marketing and engineering were consolidated, new management was hired when required, and new capital investments were made when necessary. Over time, those companies have been molded into a profitable, cohesive, growing group.

I believe that our good fortune in the area developed because we eschewed both the buccaneering financial deals and the laborious, mechanical administrative processes so familiar in industry. We move in entrepreneurial fashion. The analytical work is done by a small, closely knit group of associates who have been together for many years. We trust our judgment and we act quickly. That judgment is facilitated by the fact that we do not wander from our core business and our core knowledge. We stick to our knitting. Sometimes we have won in competition for a desirable, strategic acquisition because others did too much work up front and required approval at too many levels. The time a company loses in excessive administrative processes and presentations invariably benefits competitors who move with speed and confidence.

Of course, there is risk in moving quickly to seize an opportunity. Management is obliged to generate an effective assessment without benefit of the enormous thread of data that might make another comfortable. If the strategic fit is right, however, and if the manufacturing and engineering operations have been critically and positively reviewed, one can move quickly with confidence that the acquisition will ultimately succeed. It may take a little time, but if it makes fundamental sense, it will work.

Warren Buffett's Berkshire Hathaway clearly follows a strategy of value-driven acquisitions. I think Buffett would say that his requirements are straightforward and consistent: (1) Do not bother me with highly sophisticated technology. I want a business that is easy to understand. (2) The business must have excellent and dedicated management. (3) I must be able to buy it at a low multiple of earnings or a low multiple of cash flow. The Buffett track record over the past thirty years is impressive testament to the discipline with which he sticks to that model.

In contrast, there are the transactions designed by financial engineers. The basic idea is to use the currency of one company to buy another company that fits a financial model—strategic fit be damned. Often the suggested targets come from investment bankers who are primarily seeking transaction fees. It is easy to pick up earnings per share by using a high-priced stock with a high price-earnings ratio (that old multiple at work) to buy a company with a lower P/E. An all too familiar result is that the acquirer overpays. The overpriced stock can enrich those among the sellers who sell their newly acquired stock promptly and take the winnings off the table. In many such transactions the stock of the acquirer languishes in the twelve and twenty-four months after acquisition because, in the premium paid for the deal, he has in effect given away whatever savings the presumed synergies might have produced.

If the purpose is to build constructively through acquisition, the behavior in all too many deals belies it. The emphasis on immediate cost cutting and restructuring suggests that the deal was made for the numbers, not for the strategic value. There is surely room for financial engineers in the business world. That's just not the business I'm in, and it is vital that everyone know what business he is in.

Finally, a note on valuation. Much has been written about acquisition valuation and price, and much of that writing is useless. In a strategic acquisition, the valuation that makes sense is that one which satisfies the expectations of the two parties—the buyer and the seller. In today's sophisticated environment, the financial parameters are well known to most operators—whether they be book value, multiple of earnings (or of EBITDA), the present value of some future stream of earnings, or the dilutive impact on the acquirer's earnings. Deals seldom die because of price only. When they fail it is more often because of ignorance, arrogance, fear, or neglect. As our own Bernie Girod likes to say, "Do your homework, understand the range, then throw the stuff away and go talk to the other guy."

CHAPTER 7

Marketing and Sales: Growing a Garden

Never to make a line I have not read
in my own heart.
Yet in modesty to say, my soul
be satisfied with fruit,
with flowers, with weeds even—
But gather them in the one garden you can
truly call your own.
—*Edmond Rostand's* Cyrano de Bergerac

Marketing demands attention. Like life, it is always one thing after another. It sits atop a gathering of tectonic plates, and they keep shifting, altering the relationships among theme, packaging, negotiation, advertising, brand, and distribution.

The beauty of marketing is just that. There is no one and only right way, no standard operating procedure, no template. But its fundamental is this: Know what business you are really in.

Apple does not think it makes computers. It believes that it makes "tools for creative minds." Jet Blue doesn't behave as though it is in the airplane business. It is in the business of facilitating your life through transportation. The home theater business should be about entertainment, not about technology and gadgetry. For most of our history, Harman would say, "We are in the audio business—our products reproduce music and sound superbly." Today we say, "We are in the business of integrating many complex functions into a single, simple to use, transparent system."

KNOW YOUR CUSTOMERS

Any good marketing insight I ever generated arose from visiting and talking to customers. Jean-Marie Dru of TBWA/Chiat/Day argues, "The idea is the hero, not the customer." He quotes Henry Ford's cynical comment, "If I had asked the public what they wanted, they would have asked for a faster horse." I think not. I believe that the public would have asked for faster, more reliable transportation. Today's customer would ask for safer, more efficient, and smarter transportation.

I see the end user as the real customer. The distribution chain is only the conduit to that customer. The dealer is surely not the fellow from whom to seek product guidance. Whatever his pretensions as a marketing counselor, he is only adept at telling you what sold in that store that day. Nor is the customer the one to provide a solution or a specific product idea. That is not his discipline, nor his frame of mind. The customer, however, is the best source for learning what the need or the problem is. It is our challenge and opportunity to find the best answer to that need or to that problem.

No one ever asked for a Cuisinart before it was invented. No one asked for our high-fidelity receiver before we developed and marketed it. No one ever asked for a digital system based on the architecture of an optical bus to provide multiple services such as audible instruction navigation, voice-activated telephone, video, Internet, and MP3 access—all in a seamless, easy-to-use, integrated system. That's the solution, the answer to the question. The need and the question are available by listening to the customer. The answer and the solution are not. We as marketing anthropologists must examine the ways people live, identify their unmet needs, and design the products and services that answer the needs. The ideal is for the customer to say, "I know the question—wow, yours is the answer!" Perhaps some might add, "Why didn't I think of that?"

In the early 1950s a frequent question asked by visitors to our Harman/Kardon rooms at the high-fidelity shows was, "Why do I need all those things—that separate radio tuner, separate preamplifier, and separate power amplifier?" They knew nothing of the technical challenges to assembling all the components on a single chassis while still maintaining exemplary music reproduction. Yet when Harman/Kardon produced the first integrated receiver, free of distortion and free of mutual electrical interference among the components, it had answered the question. Similarly, as travel became more difficult, more time demanding, and more dangerous, visitors to automobile shows revealed their concerns and their needs. They were increasingly worried about safety. Could they find their way home without leaving the car? Could they keep the kids entertained through a long trip without endlessly hearing, "Are we there yet?" Could they activate and use the telephone without employing their hands? Could they engage the Internet, and could they do all of that simply and at only moderate cost? The answer to those needs was ours to develop, through the wise application of digital technology. And we did it.

Yes, marketing demands attention—attention to changes in culture and technology—attention and response to the movement of those tectonic plates. Marketing people should not begin to work only after engineering has developed the product. Marketing must be there at the beginning, to inform the effort with the implicit and explicit questions raised by the customer and to promote interaction among engineering, manufacturing, and management.

Answering customer need by employing available technology, industrial design, and distribution is the primary challenge of a company, but there are others. With that primary challenge addressed, marketing must project a possible future and then plan for it. Let us say that, after years of effort, we have finally designed a home theater system that is easy to install. It provides superior music reproduction from every available source. It incorporates a sixty-inch LCD picture for high-definition television, DVD, and satellite. It has one handsome, easy-to-use remote, which does everything, and a compact but original loudspeaker system that automatically adjusts to the acoustic peculiarities of the room. It is marketing's job to price the system and project the market size. Marketing must determine the best channel of distribution to reach the customer for whom this all-new "plug and play" system is the answer. Is the product right for today? Will it be right a year from now? If it is, do we have the accounting and service infrastructure in place to support it? If we don't, what must it be? One might argue that all this is management's job; I would agree, because I believe that marketing is a central responsibility of management.

It is great when management anticipates the future and expresses it in a new program that will arrive in time to intersect that future. It is also great to recognize the future when it is shown to you by someone else. That is what happened to me in 1995 in Karlsruhe, Germany, when engineers at Becker laid out the possibilities for a digital future.

DISTRIBUTION

Distribution is another of marketing's tectonic plates. When we started Harman/Kardon, we sold our new products to the radio parts distributors, who resold them to radio and television repairmen. We reached for the parts distributors because they had become the avenue through which public address equipment was sold. It was a channel with which we were familiar, and it was available. Soon enough, however, retail customers began to find their way to the industrial areas in which the distributors were located.

As distributor sales to retail customers increased, complaints from the radio and television servicemen grew. "We are your customers," they argued. "Why are you bypassing us?" They were indeed customers of the radio parts wholesalers, but they were not really dealers selling to consumers. They had no showrooms and carried no inventory. Conventional retail dealers for such products simply did not exist. At first the wholesalers set up showrooms in their original locations. As they drew more customers and more complaints, it was natural for them to conclude that the complaints would decline and traffic would increase if they set up stores in more traditional retail locations. Thus the first of the dedicated high-fidelity shops appeared, and reasonably soon the service trade recognized that high-fidelity retail was not really their business.

The high-fidelity stores prospered, especially in the late '50s and through the 1960s. As they developed in large cities, similar shops began to arise, especially in college towns, where a natural constituency developed among students.

In time, major national chains such as Circuit City and Best Buy were attracted to audio as a product category that suited their strategy ideally. The ticket prices and margins were relatively high, and conventional television retailers were inadequately informed or equipped to sell the products. Eventually the marketplace devolved into the major chains and those specialty retailers who maintained traction through a combination of line selection and service to the end user.

That is how it began in North America, and that is how it continues to this day. It did not begin that way in Europe. Because the primary product manufacturers were in the United States, it was easier for the American makers to sell their products in relatively larger quantities to organizations that in turn serviced the small retailers and music stores throughout Europe. Two-step distribution through established radio wholesalers became the European model.

Two-step distribution is how we marketed in Europe until just three years ago. Then it became clear that European manufacturers had developed more strength and were beginning to follow the American model of selling directly to dealers. Ours proved a clumsy, costly, and inefficient process, and we were losing ground. When we responded by changing from the two-step distribution to direct-to-dealer, our fortunes in Europe improved significantly. But there is no one absolute right mode of distribution. The best model is one that reflects history and the economics of the times. A distribution model should not be changed whimsically or capriciously, but it must be consistently reviewed and, when necessary, modified or overhauled to be relevant to the times and the company.

Although most makers of high-fidelity components have continued to market their products through a combination of specialist dealers and superstores, others have sought different channels. The Danish maker B&O (Bang & Olufsen) determined that their elegant-looking products were best marketed through dedicated B&O stores located in upscale shopping malls. Bose, another American maker, has followed multiple paths. The company continues to market through traditional retail and superstores; it also has a chain of company-owned, Bose-only shops. And it has become a master of direct mail. Their challenge is to keep three apparently conflicting channels working in reasonable peace and harmony. The move to create company-owned or franchised stores is relatively new in the field, and it is too early to judge their success. It appears to be an attractive alternative in the struggle for shelf space in traditional outlets—attractive, but very expensive. The new Apple stores reflect similar thinking in the enormously competitive personal computer business. You can bet that we and others are watching those developments with great interest.

BRANDING

Whatever the mechanism or channel of distribution may be, brand is a key marketing element in most industries, including our own. Brand seems to have its seasons. These days it is widely seen as a crucial component in any successful marketing strategy. It was not very long ago, however, that bashing brand was popular. I knew an enterprising fellow who began to market a number of commodity products, including beer and cigarettes, under the label Brand X, playing off well-known brands that contrasted their products with "Brand X" in their advertising. He simply appropriated the name, and did rather well for a while. But the idea did not have market legs. Novelties almost never do.

If brand has value, and I believe that it does, it should not be treated casually. It should not be tacked on as an afterthought to the marketing effort, and it should not be the quickly discarded victim of cost-cutting programs. It should be nourished through good times and bad. When treated as core, it will eventually pay dividends.

Brand requires patience. Recognition cannot be achieved overnight, nor will brand retain its value if inadequately attended. Legendary, powerful, dominant Coca-Cola blundered terribly decades ago when, incongruously, it introduced New Coke. Coca-Cola heralded its new drink as the product of intensive research and testing. It was pronounced the successor to the most successful soft drink in history, and one of the most successful brands ever. And it collapsed. Coke's failure came from a dreadful misreading of its own brand's value. There was no city in the world, no airport or other destination that an American traveler might reach without being greeted by a Coke billboard. Coke was surrogate for home. It had taken on the attributes of the American flag. It was embedded in the American psyche. No one should have tampered with such a brand. Build a brand and honor it. Build a brand and then respect those who are guided by it. Presume about the consumer at your peril.

Brand is emotive. If it isn't, the legion of advertisers in *Vanity*

Fair, Vogue, GQ, and *W* have it all wrong. Ralph Lauren, Gucci, Fendi, Cartier, Donna Karan, Chanel, Givenchy all picture their staggeringly attractive models in staggeringly vivid settings—and then simply sign their company names. That, they are persuaded, is what it takes. They do not offer a word of text to sell the content, the workmanship, or the more familiar specifications. "Spark the emotion, tie it to the brand, and they will come" is their marketing creed.

No one can create a brand with a single advertisement or a quick splash on television. Consider the disaster at the Super Bowl a few years ago. A gathering of dot-com wannabees invested fortunes in thirty-second and one-minute advertisements, because they remembered the compelling story and the compelling result of the original Apple Super Bowl advertisement in 1984. Something like that can happen when every star is in the right place in the firmament—but don't bet the company on it.

Brand and advertising are increasingly directed at mind share, as distinguished from market share, a distinction of growing consequence. Market share has long been the Holy Grail for many companies, and often the road to disaster. In the consumer electronics industry, it was driven by the powerful campaigns of a group of aggressive Japanese firms. Convinced that by capturing market share they would vanquish competitors and guarantee future success, those companies marketed their products vigorously outside the homeland at prices that drove competition away. The homeland and its captive marketplace would provide the company with the margin and profit necessary for survival and growth. For years the strategy succeeded. But when, inevitably, the Japanese economic bubble burst, the anchor of the program disappeared, and virtually every Japanese consumer electronics company has since struggled just to stay afloat.

Mind share is very different. It speaks to capturing the emotion and commitment of the individual customer. There is no more effective route to that mind than a splendid product, effectively branded and effectively advertised.

With regard to advertising, make sure first that you know what you are talking about. If there is copy, the copy must be authentic. Since we try to persuade the other fellow to see the truth as we see it, we had better believe it ourselves if we want to be believed. Miss the rhythm, misuse the word, appear to be out of your element, and you lose that audience whose respect is crucial and whose devotion you seek.

Because the pace of life is so fast and the attention span of audiences is so short, advertising has moved increasingly to depend on the emotive phrase, the emotive image. That phrase must capture essence; that image must rivet the attention and provoke the response in a moment. It is no easy task and, even as some children's doodling may imitate art, an occasional hit is not good enough. Billboards and magazines are full of word and picture imagery that leave the audience baffled, confused, or uninterested. By contrast, the occasional "Think Different" or "Drivers Wanted" can be compelling and unforgettable, and the percentage of observers who connect the phrase to the product is impressively high.

Harman advertising has always reflected the state of the public's awareness of the high-fidelity product. As that awareness has grown, the need for text to explain its role or to advocate its special virtues has diminished. I believe that advertising should do more than sell the particular product. It should also and always sell the company and its character. The purpose should be to build continuing commitment by the customer to the company so that every product purchase is, in effect, an investment in the company. Our goal has been to create a customer for life.

I remember to this day our earliest advertising efforts. In the early 1950s, I found myself in the company of musicians and composers. In his late years, the great Duke Ellington discovered us and enjoyed what we were doing. In his last months he would talk with me from his hospital bed almost daily. Those visits led me to our first Harman ad. I bought a full page in the *New York Times Magazine*. As I recall, it cost only seven hundred dollars then. The advertisement pictured the Duke at the piano in a dramatic chiaroscuro photograph. Its headline read, "The Duke was Made for High Fidelity." The text suggested that our products provided the opportunity to hear him virtually live in your home.

Shortly thereafter, CBS television did a pioneering broadcast of the United Nations as it celebrated its first anniversary in its new headquarters in Manhattan. Pablo Casals, the great cellist, had returned from self-exile in Puerto Rico to conduct a concert honoring the UN. After he had completed it, and CBS had broadcast it live to its television audience, celebrated journalist

Daniel Schorr interviewed the maestro under a hot sun outside the building.

"Tell me, maestro," asked Daniel Schorr, "why, in this first celebration of the assembly of many nations and many cultures, did you choose a program that was entirely Johann Sebastian Bach?" Casals looked up at Schorr with a tear glistening on his cheek. "Why not?" he asked. "Bach is my best friend."

I was really touched. I commissioned a friend to do a sketch of Casals, bent over his cello as he sat in a small wicker chair. Using that sketch, I ran an ad in the *New York Times* headlined "Bach is My Best Friend." The text suggested how he could become yours.

We continue to celebrate the artistry of great musicians in our advertising. The connection serves us well. My awareness of their work and the friendships I have developed with many of them, including such artistic giants as Yo-Yo Ma, Beverly Sills, and Wynton Marsalis, not only inform our advertising, they inform my life.

Literate advertising, emotive messages, authentic text, and crisp illustrations of the product have been our guide over the years. These days the emphasis is more on the spirit and the brand, and less on detailed product description. They usually include illustrations of recognizable artists—Santana, Sills, Marsalis—eyes closed, expressions of joy and reverence as they listen to the music, counterpointed by a similar expression on the face of a young, anonymous listener. Such images, and our brand signature, have served us well over the years.

It is difficult to create and maintain successful brands. Virtually every one of the other pioneer names in high fidelity has disappeared or is in decline. Fisher, Pilot, HH Scott, Jensen, and others who emerged and grew alongside us have largely disappeared.

Keeping our brands alive and vigorous has made them valuable to the automakers. A number of them offer our premium branded high-fidelity systems as options in their cars. The use of our brand authenticates the quality of their system and arguably the quality of the entire vehicle, and reassures the consumer who is asked to pay a premium for it. As the carmakers learned that there is significant profit to be made by featuring our systems in their cars, and as increasing numbers of consumers reached for the opportunity to make the car a traveling music salon, our brands found wheels.

At the beginning, and for some years, we believed (and they agreed) that each automaker should promote its own exclusive, respected audio brand: Infinity for Chrysler, JBL for Toyota, and Mark Levinson for Lexus. Today, Harman/Kardon is moving beyond that manufacturers' exclusive model as it becomes a generic symbol of quality and design for audio. Today, Mercedes, BMW, Audi, Saab, and Buick all embrace it. Apple employs it in their new Macs and Toshiba in their vaunted laptops. In effect, each now claims Harman/Kardon as its stamp of audio authenticity.

For us, there is a sweet circular quality to all of this. It starts with the now traditional home products, which endorse and confirm the systems in the cars and computers, and those millions of quality images on the road and on desks in turn enhance the brand.

Automakers today are moving to completely integrated systems that combine information and entertainment functions. The challenge to us is this: shall we accept the view that Harman/Kardon, JBL, Infinity, and Mark Levinson are now and forever audio brands, and that we must somehow develop a new brand for the larger engagement? It is not an easy question, and it is surely not unique to our company. Is there something precise and limited about a brand's reach? Is Apple a computer brand, incapable of being anything more? Is the Nike effort to reach beyond running shoes and shorts to golf equipment and balls too early to judge? Is the Yves Saint Laurent disaster a warning about expanding the reach of a brand, or does it merely caution about proceeding indiscriminately?

The Ralph Lauren brand has moved successfully from clothing to embrace household furnishings and interiors; IBM has moved successfully from computing hardware alone to software system solutions. I am convinced that we, too, must find ways to extend our brands' reach to match our understanding and definition of our business.

SALES

I enjoy marketing, and I enjoy selling as well. They are not the same, but I think of them as intimately related. Marketing is the larger picture. It provides the overall framework, the strategic direction. It engages the tools of market research and interpreted data. If marketing is strategic, selling is tactical.

I learned long ago that if you can persuade the other fellow to accept the harmonics of an idea or an argument, the fundamental will somehow be assumed—and the sale made. It is a procedure employed by the effective automobile salesman who at the right moment asks, "What color will you take it in?" If the prospect answers, "I'll take it in blue," he has answered the implicit question, "Will you buy the car?" If the discussion about a cruise is turned to a review of the entertainment to be experienced on board, the client has essentially agreed to go.

In 1955, as I was barnstorming in an effort to create dealerships for Harman/Kardon's new kind of product, I stopped at a small bicycle shop in Peoria, Illinois. It was my first child's birthday and I was eager to buy her a new bicycle, although I knew it would prove an expensive urge. The owner of the store introduced "the perfect bicycle for your kid." He extolled its virtues, the solidity of the frame, the suppleness of its leather seat, the assurance implicit in the sturdy handles, the ride, the tires, and the powerful spokes. He rhapsodized about the four-gear shift, the new transmission system, and the brilliant headlamp. I could not wait for him to finish. He had sold me—absolutely. But then, when he had completed his poetic presentation and I was ready to say "Wrap it up," he added, "And to get you to buy it, I'm willing to knock 20 percent off the price." I was totally deflated—and tempted not to buy. When the product and the presentation have value, the good salesman knows when to stop and close the sale. When the presentation has been persuasive, there is no reason to give the product away.

In September 2002, I made the keynote talk at the annual convention of the Custom Electronics Design and Installation Association in Minneapolis. CEDIA is the most rapidly developing expression of the high-fidelity industry. CEDIA dealers do not have storefronts and do not carry inventory. They are designers of multifunctional home entertainment centers that include music, video, movies, lighting, and security. Each such system is a virtual prototype because it is tailored to the particular home and the particular customer. Because the systems are multifunctional and serve many rooms, the rooms are equipped with keypads to select the desired entertainment. All of this makes for relatively complex systems.

The field has been growing at an exponential rate, and more than a thousand members came to hear the talk. I argued that the opportunities for their developing industry were unnecessarily limited because the systems they produced were frequently far too complicated and difficult to use. This complexity leaves many customers overwhelmed and disenchanted. It causes far too many operating failures, and too many operating failures provoke too many unpaid-for service calls. It is not the way to build a profitable business. I cautioned them to avoid doing something only because it is technically possible. The emphasis should be on satisfying real need. Were that done consistently, I urged, large amounts of their time would be freed to do more selling of new systems. More buyers would be content, and more of those buyers would promote their service. Some disagreed, because they were convinced that the genius of their business lay in that very complexity. So few can really put those systems together, they insisted, the customer must come to us. I am sure that they are wrong. The future belongs to those who make the complex simple. I am reassured because a number of dealers have contacted me since to express appreciation for the insight. The subject of my speech, "Every Customer a Salesman," sounds to them like an excellent objective.

Selling is rarely seen these days in terms of Arthur Miller's Willy Loman. The good old boy, the hail-fellow-well-met is essentially a thing of the past. And it is a good thing. When properly practiced, selling is an art form. It requires knowledge of the product and knowledge of the customer, and it invites a sense of social responsibility. Beware the salesman who "can sell ice to the Eskimos." The good salesman is one who serves the customer's real need, and by doing so creates another advocate for the product.

There is an old joke about the fellow who walks into a store and sees shelf after shelf loaded with bags of salt. "That's a lot of salt," the visitor says. "You think that's a lot of salt," says the store owner, "come with me—I'll show you salt." Down the steps to the basement they go, and there, rack after rack as far as the eye can see—nothing but bags of salt. "You must sell a heck of a lot of salt," the visitor observes. The owner replies, "I don't sell much salt. You should see the fellow who sold it to me. He sells salt!"

The effective salesman knows that when he sells product to a distribution organization or a store, he is only serving a conduit. Nothing meaningful happens until that product is eventually bought by a consumer. The perspective that the distributor or the store is the customer will time and again lead to failure. The successful salesperson is successful, in part, because he understands that such a sale is only the beginning. It isn't real until a live consumer says "Wrap it up," and it isn't concluded until that customer is happy with the purchase.

CHAPTER 8

WEIGHING EDUCATION, GOVERNMENT, AND BUSINESS

Where is the wisdom we have lost in knowledge?
Where is the knowledge we have lost in information?
—*T. S. ELIOT,* CHORUSES FROM "THE ROCK"

CIVIL RIGHTS AND EDUCATION

In 1955 the Supreme Court ruled that "separate but equal" schools were unconstitutional and that desegregation of public schools must proceed "with all deliberate speed." After many lengthy legal delays, Prince Edward County in Virginia chose in the late summer of 1959 to thwart the Court's decision by shutting down its public school system. It then created the Prince

Edward Academy, a private school open only to white students. The awful result was that for four years, no black children in Prince Edward County received any formal education.

In 1962, as the civil rights movement was beginning to gather strength, and after the Freedom Rider buses had traveled through the South, Dr. Martin Luther King visited Prince Edward County. I had met Dr. King earlier that year because of my growing interest in civil rights and through my friendship with Harry Wachtel, his attorney. King criticized the community for its inhuman treatment of young, innocent Americans and urged action to end the county's indifference. I would not see him again until the day before his assassination in Memphis, where I had gone to join his march in support of the city's sanitation workers.

Shortly after Dr. King's visit to Prince Edward County, President Kennedy spoke of the crisis there in a message to Congress. Then in March 1963, Robert Kennedy spoke at the Kentucky Centennial Celebration of the Emancipation Proclamation. He said:

> We may observe with much sadness and irony that, outside of Africa, south of the Sahara, where education is still a difficult challenge, the only places on earth known not to provide free public education are communist China, North Vietnam, Sarawak, Singapore, British Honduras—and Prince Edward County, Virginia. Something must be done about Prince Edward County.

That something was the organization by the Kennedy administration of the Prince Edward County Free School Association.

My friend Bill vanden Heuvel was charged by the attorney general to oversee the project, and Dr. Neil Sullivan, who had been superintendent of schools in New England, was appointed its superintendent. They encouraged me to join them, and I was eager to do so. For eleven glorious months our school was the Camelot of education. We loved it and the kids loved it. I flew to Richmond at my own expense each week to teach there. The trip from the airport to the town of Farmville, Virginia, where I lodged with a black family, was always harrowing. The car was trailed, bumped, and harassed—and I was often frightened. But the school was wonderful; the classes I taught, and my uncashed paycheck, stay with me these decades later.

One class was in American history, which I tried to teach from the perspective of a black person in the South. Frederick Douglass, the great journalist/activist, was my model, and his writing was my source. Eight students comprised the small senior class. They ranged in age from eighteen to twenty-six. We were twenty-five miles from historic Appomattox, where the Civil War had finally ended, and not one of those students had ever heard of it. The second class was titled "Sidney's Aesthetics," and it brought a large crowd into the auditorium each week. There we read and interpreted poetry, listened to my music and theirs on a player I brought with me, played at architecture, and wondered about humor and what it was that made us laugh.

The school flourished and the kids were happy. Puzzled at first by the fact that almost none of them knew their surnames, I came finally to realize that the only reason I knew mine in my early days at school was that I was obliged to answer when attendance was taken. When you're out of school for years, there's little need to respond to a roll call.

I was sitting on the back porch of the school building, chatting with Neil Sullivan, when we saw a wild plume of dust raised by a speeding car as it took the back road to the building. The driver was bringing the news that President John Kennedy had that day, November 22, 1963, been assassinated in Dallas. As word spread through the building, the kids poured out of the classrooms on their own tears. Kennedy had been their hero, and the world would never be the same.

Prince Edward County played a significant part in America's struggle for civil rights. I was honored to have been a part of it. Today the county is the primary beneficiary of our effort, which was part of a massive and historic movement. Its public schools, finally reopened in 1964, are fully integrated, and those schools produce a disproportionate number of National Merit Scholars.

AN EDUCATION IN EDUCATION

Neil Sullivan moved from Prince Edward County to become superintendent of the District 2 Board of Education on Long Island, New York. In 1965, I was elected president of the board. By that time I had four children attending school there, and I was hopeful that my excitement about learning would infect them. The district and its Wheatley High School have long been considered among the very best public schools in the country. Our board of education was committed to the development of the schools and, equally important, to the engagement of the community as an active participant in the education of their kids. An essay on education, which I wrote that year, was distributed widely by the school district. Its theme was that our job was to graduate wise men—not wise guys, that our emphasis must be on learning rather than on just how to get through the school and how to pass its examinations. It read, in part:

> What really is the purpose of education in our District? We believe that students cannot be regarded merely as vessels to be filled with information and to be tested from time to time to determine how well that information is contained. There must be a broad objective, philosophically rooted, which gives meaning to education in terms of what the student does with it and how it serves to complete the "whole man." This goes beyond the thought of secondary school as nothing more than a stepping stone to college. It thinks of it as part of the continuum of learning and of the application of learning that moves through life in the period following formal education.

> [Our] educational program measures itself in terms of how well this is accomplished. It recognizes and promotes the students' awareness that with judgment making goes the responsibility for those judgments.

> This, it might be argued, is the path to wisdom, that composite of knowledge, value, and human warmth which contrasts sharply with the more routine process of acquiring information.

When my tour as president of the board ended, Dr. Sullivan urged me to become familiar with a new college that had been formed on Long Island, sponsored by the Quakers, the Society of Friends. Neil said that the views I had developed in Prince Edward County and honed in the Long Island School District were in full flower at the college. I accepted his guidance and presented myself to Morris Mitchell, then president of Friends World College. That great man, disciple of the legendary educator John Dewey, unfolded his giant frame from the chair in which he was sitting and, dwarfing me, explained that if I wanted to teach at the school, I must first serve an apprenticeship. He defined the apprenticeship as service on the board of trustees. I joined him and had served for three years when, sadly, Morris Mitchell succumbed to cancer.

The board, to my astonishment, asked me to succeed him. My acceptance ushered in the wildest three years of my life. Fully absorbed by the effort to lead the school and also run Harman International, I was at it day and night every day of every week. It was totally demanding and totally rewarding.

Friends World College's thinking was influenced by the work of two revolutionary scholars, Ivan Illich in Mexico and Paolo Freire in Brazil. In his seminal book *Deschooling Society*, Illich described conventional education's dependency on professionals who "control how we learn and how we don't." He proposed a new model in which people would be in charge of their own learning. Freire had been minister of education in Brazil until the military overthrew the reform-minded Goulart regime in 1964. Freire had experienced extraordinary success in teaching illiterate peasants to read and write in as short a time as thirty hours. I was intrigued and stimulated by the teaching of the two scholars, each of whom gave great weight to dialogue.

The college was headquartered in Northampton, Long Island. There were centers in seven other countries including Mexico, Great Britain, India, Africa, and China. The operative idea was that each student would enter the college at the center closest to home and then travel serially around the world, spending one semester in each of the other seven centers. The final semester would be spent studying back at home. The program would produce a multinational, multilingual, multicultural student body in each center—an environment, we were confident, that would be highly stimulative to original thinking and a growing appetite for learning.

During that wild three-year period, I spent time at the centers in Mexico, London, India, and Africa. Each confirmed the potential in the concept, and in each a number of students wrote stunning journals. The level of original writing exceeded anything I had ever encountered when I was in school.

As a student, this was material I had yearned for. I had slipped through high school virtually unnoticed and was fortunate to have earned admission to New York's vaunted tuition-free City College. I soon connected to an unofficial college underground that had blossomed at New York University. There, student participants created an exciting alternative to formal, higher education. Self-directed, we explored what we really wished to learn. Inspired by the unsupervised and undirected search for knowledge, I discovered T. S. Eliot, Kierkegaard, Shakespeare, Tolstoy,

Voltaire, Brahms, Mozart—and critical judgment. The formal part of my education was surely junior to the marvelous journey at unofficial New York University.

I did not realize, until writing of it, how much that journey informed my thinking at Friends World College and, through FWC, my approach to business and the workplace. The great anthropologist Margaret Mead liked to say that she was reared by her grandmother "who wanted me to be an educated person, so, of course, she kept me out of school."

AN EDUCATION IN GOVERNMENT

As I wrote in chapter 2, it was Friends World College that led me to the work experiment in Bolivar, Tennessee. That experiment in altering the workplace environment caught the attention of a number of journalists around the country and, in particular, the editor of the Nashville newspaper *The Tennessean*. He dispatched Al Gore, Jr., at the time a young reporter, to write a series of articles about it. The articles caught the attention of the new vice president elect of the United States, Walter Mondale. Mondale spoke of them to the president-elect, Jimmy Carter, and I was invited to come to D.C. There I was offered the position of deputy secretary of commerce.

With no political or government experience, I arrived in Washington in stunning innocence. I reached back to my time at the Officer Candidate School and committed myself once again to making it work. Making it work proved a mix of hells and benefits. One sweet benefit in my very first week was meeting Jane Frank in the Roosevelt Room of the White House. Jane was then deputy to the secretary to the Cabinet. One of her responsibilities was to write the minutes of each Monday morning Cabinet meeting I came to those meetings in awe of my proximity to the president and persuaded that my comments must be brief and insightful. A few years ago the former president made a gift to me of a set of those meeting minutes. I was astonished to note that my brief interventions had somehow grown in length and dominated the minutes of every session I attended.

Jane and I married four years after our first meeting. President Carter claims personal credit for our now twenty-five years together.

Charged with staffing most of the senior positions in the vast Department of Commerce, I converted the exercise to a learning experience. I chose the assistant secretary for technology as my first appointment. Since I knew nothing about technology in government, I used my lofty new office to contact the most senior scientists in the country. All were helpful. Some, including Lewis Branscomb, then chief scientist at mighty IBM, helped me identify a number of marvelously qualified candidates. I assembled them in Washington at what I labeled a seminar.

Through the discussion, one person emerged as the most impressive, Jordan Baruch. He accepted my job offer and became our Assistant Secretary for Science and Technology. Thereafter I conducted interviews for the other major posts in the department in the same manner.

Commerce was an unbelievable collection of agencies. I

would challenge anyone to name them all. It then included (I think it still does) the Census Bureau, ITA (International Trade Administration), Bureau of Standards, National Aquarium, NOAA (National Oceanographic and Atmospheric Administration), and EDA (Economic Development Agency), among many others. With over sixty thousand employees, I was challenged to serve as its chief operating officer. To help me know it better, I assigned myself to work at each of the agencies for a period of three days to a week in the role of midlevel bureaucrat. I learned first that, unlike the frequent caricatures of the bloated, lazy bureaucrat, the vast majority of those who worked in government were bright, hardworking, and stunningly patriotic. Most of them could easily have found better-paying jobs in industry. They wanted to serve the nation. Because I never arrived with an adjutant or photographer, the people in the agencies quickly took me at my word. I was there for serious work. Time and again, however, I heard the same plea, "I do not know where the material I work on comes from, and I do not know where the product of my work goes." That is a prescription for frustration and alienation, and I worked hard to change the work situation.

In early 1977, Washington became totally absorbed by shoes. The shoe industry consisted for the most part of small, privately held companies with annual sales in the $2 to $10 million range. Typically they were run by second- or third-generation descendants of the family founders and were located in no fewer than thirty-two states. For some years the Commerce Department had been processing applications for financial assistance from companies and discharged employees who claimed to have been adversely affected by unfair foreign competition. We called it "trade adjustment assistance." Labor called it "burial assistance."

When the industry found itself in deep trouble because of rising competition from Singapore, Korea, Indonesia, and Italy, the new president was besieged by as many as sixty-four senators. They had concluded that the health of the industry was central to the nation's survival. To deflect the pressure of the industry and its senatorial supporters, the beleaguered president sent them "to see that fellow in the Department of Commerce who claims to know something about business. I am sure he can help you." I was that fellow. You can well imagine the lack of enthusiasm, indeed the hostility, with which the principals in those shoe companies came to see me. They wanted trade embargoes and border relief. They got me. Still, I brought some of the entrepreneurial thinking that my years at Bogen and Harman had shaped. I identified people in various departments of the government who had experience that matched the needs of the majority of the troubled companies—and we knew who those companies were because they had applied for trade adjustment assistance.

I learned quickly that some of the small companies knew how to make a very good product, but had absolutely no idea how to cost or price it. Some knew how to make it and how to price it, but were bereft of any ability to market and sell it. There were many who knew how to do all of that, but were totally incapable of manufacturing in a reasonably efficient fashion. I identified the approximately 150 troubled firms and assembled a dozen teams from different departments of government (each included a marketing person, an accounting specialist, and a knowledgeable production person); I put the teams in touch with the shoemakers, their new clients. Because I had assembled so many competitors in one industry, I was obliged to worry about antitrust matters. Fortunately, I persuaded the attorney general to direct two of his antitrust lawyers to sit in on our meetings and help guide the conversations so that, while they were constructive, they also stayed within the law.

The program worked remarkably well. Our teams had the time of their lives. It sure beat much of the humdrum work in government, and numbers of those small shoe companies were indeed revived. So successful were we that when the Reagan administration came to town four years later, it announced that we had done our job. The old-line shoe industry had been revived and the program was no longer necessary. It was dissolved.

I thought that judgment was incorrect and the action premature. Still, we saw valuable results and learned some important lessons. One, there is a place for original, unorthodox thinking in government. Two, the shoe program confirmed that one of the dumbest things you can utter is, "This is the way we've always done it," implicitly, "This is the way we will always do it." It ain't necessarily so and it doesn't necessarily follow.

Working on new programs was exciting and rewarding. Getting along in the government was often another matter. It seemed to me that Washington was an assembly of the most remarkably smart people in the country—all gathered to make certain that nothing happened.

Consider how the executive branch develops new legislation

to propose. The subject usually arises in the White House, where it has been introduced by one of the departments of government. Soon enough, a meeting of the principals—the department secretaries—is held to scope the matter. Once that meeting has been concluded, a second meeting of less senior figures is convened to initiate the working sessions. Rarely if ever do any of the participants come to that meeting without instructions that the prerogatives and the holy turf of their departments must not be compromised. It is all too often the primary focus. It must be evident that such a process tends to reach conclusions that offend no one and cut no new ground.

Little wonder twenty-five years later that the process of creating the new Department of Homeland Security in 2002 generated so much heat, so much dissonance, and so much delay, even though the subject was absolutely crucial to the nation's future. The largest federal reorganization since the Department of Defense was formed in 1947 engaged four senior White House aides, operating in secret. Congress then created a special committee to oversee the effort, or its own turf battles would surely derail it. That almost happened despite the committee.

It remains to be seen how effectively twenty-two separate agencies can be merged into the Department of Homeland Security or whether congressional oversight will support or strangle the effort. It is a mighty wonder that anything of real consequence ever emerges from such a process. Still, to paraphrase Winston Churchill, however faulty it may be, it is the best process that democratic society has yet created.

In several ways, government and higher education were sim-

161

ilar experiences for me. In government, it was the civil servants who were my joy, as the key senior appointees fought their turf wars. At the college, the faculty and trustees were the ones who kept me awake at night as they fussed about their tenure, their privilege, and their power. There, the students were the easy part.

It is commonplace to hear people in government observe that "the difference between this and business is that there is no bottom line in government." That really says a lot. The presence of that bottom line is always a goad to businesspeople to get something done, to bring the matter to conclusion. Other than for a crisis, a similar goad and discipline do not exist in government.

I was troubled by the turf wars in government, and they were not unique to the Carter administration. They go with the territory in any administration. I was no less troubled by the implicit view many senior government employees seemed to hold that "We could run such a lovely government if we didn't have to be bothered with the people."

Higher education often gathers a crowd of prima donnas who are forever checking each other and their perquisites. Learning should be paramount and wisdom should be the objective, but both are often shortchanged in a highly politicized environment.

After all is said and done, my sense is that although frequently scorned and sometimes exploited by dishonest managers, business is in most respects the straightest and the most reasonable of the three areas. It is the one that provides the most unfettered opportunities for creativity, originality, experimentation, collegiality, and human and social development.

CHAPTER 9

SIDNEY'S ALMANAC

The heart of a fool is in his mouth,
but the mouth of a wise man is
in his heart.
Here comes the orator
with his flood of words and
his drop of reason.
—*BENJAMIN FRANKLIN,*
POOR RICHARD'S ALMANAC

Upon rereading this book, I have considered what I have drawn from the experience of writing it. My reflections are embodied in the following paragraphs—my Almanac.

ON DEVELOPING A PERSONAL COMPASS

If an executive has no higher responsibility than the exercise of his convictions and the setting of an example for others, he had better know what he believes in, for to know what you believe in is to equip yourself to handle opportunity, challenge, or disappointment with assurance.

Getting to know what you believe in is tough work. But once you've done it, challenges that once seemed insuperable lend themselves to solution. Disappointment or failure can be placed in perspective and opportunity can be attacked with enthusiasm.

The process starts best with the recognition that one needs a personal compass—that it is aimless to proceed without a road map. Without one we are obliged to travel blind, to feel our way for the answers. Too few of us trouble to clarify, organize, and ultimately codify and articulate what attributes and values we hold dear. Are they honesty, courage, consistency, respect for others? Do they include brevity, curiosity, enthusiasm?

The early Greeks distinguished human beings from other forms of life in terms of our ability to contemplate our actions and to consider their consequences. They called it praxis. Too many people do not engage in praxis—they may read, they may observe, they may listen to a sermon, but they do not consciously lay out the grid of their beliefs.

For me, life is exciting and rewarding when I am mentally and physically alert. I work at both parts. I work to develop and improve particular skills: writing, speaking, physical stamina, the exercise of curiosity, and the ability to succeed financially.

I choose fairness and personal development—my own, my colleagues', and my constituents'—over personal financial enrichment. I judge that something is good or bad depending on whether it supports those objectives. I have persuaded myself that if I pursue such a path, I will successfully and constructively fulfill my obligations to shareholders, stakeholders, investors in our business, my family—and myself.

And I am convinced that personal courage will be a by-product of such an attitude toward development. People have said of me that I have "balls"—that I am effective under pressure. If that's so, I am certain it arises from entering any event with a codified set of values and beliefs. It is reinforced by exercising careful judgment, and by the conviction that I know what I am doing. I'm not just aimlessly making my way. I am instead setting a reasoned course. I am prepared to accommodate new information and changed circumstances, and act accordingly. By proceeding honorably and enthusiastically, and with energy and determination, I will improve the odds. If it all works—good! If it does not, I am prepared to fold my cards and walk away. My inner compass will surely guide me to another worthwhile undertaking.

IMPROVING THE ODDS

Although I have written of this earlier, I think it worth expanding, because a business deal or investment—the purchase of a house, or the playing of a round of golf—all present handicaps, hurdles, and challenges. There is usually another bidder, often hidden risks, and, in golf, the variables in swing, weather, opponents, and courage. Rather than thinking about the matter in absolute terms—"I must win or I lose"—I suggest that the odds, unguided, favor a loss.

Improving the odds is first cousin to Václav Havel's distinction between hope and optimism, and to my own distinction between daring and recklessness. Each suggests that life, work, business, family, and golf are not zero-sum games. You do not necessarily lose if you don't win. A far better approach is to understand the calculus of the matter, to prepare thoroughly, to recognize and reckon with the barriers, and then to proceed.

The fact that some lucky few bring nothing to the work but still thrive teaches us only that they are accidents of chance. What we don't see are the hundreds, the thousands, indeed the hundreds of thousands of such folk who never get past the entrance. One should ignore the lucky few who do and waste no time hoping to be one of them. Since the odds are naturally pretty poor, we should do all the things we can to improve them. Then, go for it. If you succeed, wonderful! If not, you gave it your best effort. And when you have a thoughtfully, honestly developed personal compass, the odds for success are significantly better—not for one event or one game or one experiment—but for life.

ON WRITING

Sadly, writing is lightly regarded in business and often dismissed as unnecessary. Executives frequently declaim, "I do not write.

I'm a people person. I like to look the other fellow in the eye." That's a clever rationalization. There is a time to look the other fellow in the eye, of course, but writing is a unique and powerful instrument. The familiar assumption is that it consists of transferring fully formed intellectual inventory from the mind to the page. But that is not so! Writing is discovery. Anyone who has done any serious writing has experienced the surprise that comes when reading in the morning that which he wrote the night before. The reaction is often, "This is remarkable. I did not know I knew that." As I noted in the foreword, the great Welsh poet Dylan Thomas spoke of "the blank page on which I read my mind." The person who invests in writing, who exercises the discipline to do it well, and who uses it frequently, will possess a matchless instrument for discovery, clarity, and persuasion.

Most business schools seem to share the same dismal view of writing that is common in business. It is rarely treated as a major tool to be developed and honed. At least implicitly, the B-schools join in industry's disregard.

In 1998, I endowed the Writer-in-Residence program at the Baruch School of Business in New York City. It invites notable writers and poets to spend time at the college engaging the students and encouraging appreciation for and involvement in writing. Tony Kushner and Edward Albee, among others, have participated and sung its praises. The program has generated unexpectedly high levels of student interest, and these days it is always oversubscribed. That tells me something about the intrinsic appeal of writing.

My own experience persuades me that it is the most over-

167

looked skill in the business arena, and one that rewards the executive in many ways. It helps clarify one's thinking. It improves all other means of communication by enhancing vocabulary and promoting the ability to formulate thoughts in coherent and creative ways. It is first cousin to public speaking, because it helps frame the material in a fashion that makes it explicable and communicable. That is essential in public speaking.

Writing, like public speaking, does not come easily. You must invest in it. You must tolerate frustration and disappointment. You must persevere. Everyone has writer's block when making that first effort. But hanging in and learning from one effort to the next pays dividends. It will come as no surprise that I have promoted writing at Harman. Today in our company virtually every executive of any consequence writes. I would wager that virtually all of them agree that it is one of the most productive skills they have acquired at the company.

ON PUBLIC SPEAKING AND STORYTELLING

When a senior business officer addresses a gathering of analysts, shareholders, or potential customers, the ability to speak directly makes a big difference. Talk without notes and the voice becomes authentic. It is not unusual for someone who does that well to be approached by members of the audience who comment, "You didn't even use notes." After all, if a speech is to be read, one might just as well send to central casting for a handsome person with a sonorous voice to read it. When you speak directly to them, an audience pays attention. "The speaker is looking at me. I don't dare yawn or let my attention drift."

I always have a solid idea of what I wish to say before I move to the microphone; I may well have notes that I review before I talk. Then I keep them in my pocket. After the talk I can check the notes and determine how much of what I intended to say I remembered to, and how much I may have forgotten. Whenever I score 60 percent or better, I rate that a success, and the more of it I do, the higher that percentage becomes.

Just as unaided public speaking is a tremendous tool, so too is storytelling. Audiences and individuals always respond to a good story well told. A story of one's personal experience, when it is relevant, can be more influential, more compelling, than any other form of communication. Here's a story borrowed from Arthur Miller's *Death of a Salesman*:

Willy Loman, the protagonist of the play, has come to the office of his former neighbor, the attorney, seeking a handout. The attorney is closeted with a client and Willy must wait in the reception room. The attorney's son arrives and joins Willy. He is carrying a briefcase and a tennis racket, and he and Willy visit. When, eventually, the attorney completes his meeting and joins them in the reception room, he turns to Willy and, pointing at his son, asks, "What do you think of that boy? Do you know that tomorrow morning he will plead a case before the Supreme Court of the United States of America?" Willy is aghast. "We talked for forty minutes. He never mentioned it." The father responds, "Willy, he doesn't have to mention it. He's doing it."

Told at a propitious moment, such a story makes a telling

point. It argues for modesty, it suggests that someone who recites it probably honors its message, and it makes clear, by reference, that the storyteller draws guidance from a respected, valuable source.

Storytelling is especially useful when addressing an audience. It can illustrate, it can entertain, and it can hold their attention. The listeners may tease you about the storytelling or the recitation of relevant poetry, but they nearly always admire it and wonder, "How does he do it?"

Jack Valenti is a superb public speaker. In his book, *Speak Up with Confidence: How to Prepare, Learn, and Deliver Effective Speeches,* Jack recommends that the executive memorize the closing paragraph of his talk. That's fine if the purpose is to conclude the talk with something direct, personal, and dramatic. After all, if you have read the entire talk up to that point, you need something personal to wrap it up. I suggest that it is far better to read no part of the talk, and to present it in what appears to be total spontaneity. That way, by the time you get to the closing, you know what you plan to say and it will come across as authentic. Knowing is very different from memorizing. Memorizing usually comes off as memorized.

ON THINKING

Sylvia Harman and I divorced in 1970 after twenty-five years of marriage and four lovely children. We were unable to overcome the tension and pressures in our marriage generated by my 24/7 days while running Harman International and Friends World College. I lived the life of a single man for the next ten years and married Jane in 1980. We maintained a cordial relationship with Sylvia until, sadly, she died a year ago. Sylvia, in noting the differences between us, once said to me, "I have a think switch in my brain. When I have something to think about, I turn the switch on. When I have finished thinking about it, I turn it off. You, Sidney, either do not have a think switch or, if you do, it was locked in the ON position at birth."

I did not know whether she intended it as a compliment or criticism, but I have considered it many times since, and have decided that for me the switch is indeed locked in the ON position. That doesn't mean that I never relax or that I am always engaged, but it does mean that thinking is not a process I turn to only when I judge it necessary. It goes on all the time. And it should.

Many people, it seems to me, do not engage their thoughts except when they decide—"Now I must!" As a result, many a conversation or discussion is quite undisciplined; it wanders around, on the assumption that somehow something may come of it. I don't consider thinking as sport. I have no affection for debate as an exercise, but I have trained myself to come at a subject in an organized way. If the opportunity is there to anticipate the discussion, I do think it through. I automatically ask myself the purpose of the exchange. What do we want this discussion to produce? Is it a solution or a point of view; is it how to write a thank-you note or, for that matter, a note of condolence? Whatever it may be, I don't engage it without some preparation. That preparation borrows from and depends on my entire history. What is it that I can use for guidance; how can I, from previous experience, synthesize a position in this matter? It is not the same as borrowing whole the experience of another conversation. It is rather a matter of engaging previous experience to inform the new, the present.

Then I measure the idea against the values, the standards, the moral/ethical base I have developed for myself. It needs to fit; it needs to stand up to that review. With a point of view developed, I consider how to present it and I tell myself what I wish to accomplish. Is it concurrence or agreement from someone else? Is it concession or acceptance? Is it discovery? Is it a willingness to be persuaded to a new viewpoint, or is it the seeking of an answer neither party brought to the conversation? If I do not have an idea about the purpose and the target, I increase the likelihood of a rambling, incoherent, inconclusive exchange.

No matter what the nature of the conversation, I start with some objective and some organization in mind. In the absence of such an approach, the exchange will likely lead to nothing. Two centuries ago, Talleyrand observed that man was given language to disguise his thoughts. Kierkegaard demurred. He insisted that man was given language to disguise the fact that he doesn't have any thoughts. I suppose I disagree with both. Talleyrand was cynical, Kierkegaard unflattering. One should have thoughts. They should be reasonably considered then expressed directly, crisply, and clearly.

When I am about to express a thought, I use a practice I trained myself in as a youngster. I edit what I am about to say a microsecond before I say it. The practice is now so instinctive that I can reasonably say, I don't even think about it. It just happens and it saves me time and again from saying something inappropriate, something stupid, or something incorrect.

Years ago I joined a meeting conducted by the recently appointed head of marketing. When I heard him refer to a newly developed product with the comment, "Now that it is fully functional, we must hang a pretty dress on the pig," I thought I would die. That man's tongue clearly outran his brain, and I knew for certain he would not make it.

When Louis V. Gerstner, Jr., who did a superb job of reshaping, redirecting, and reinvigorating the stumbling IBM, said at his first news conference, "The last thing IBM needs is a vision," he meant that there was an enormous amount of hardcore work he had to get done and that everyone else had to get done before they could turn to a new perspective. It is clear that early in his tenure he did generate a very clear vision and that he steered IBM superbly down a path away from disaggregated hardware to "solutions for a small planet." Nonetheless, I would wager that if he could do it over again, he would not say "the last thing" in that situation. He has been obliged to spend too many hours defending or explaining the comment ever since.

ON EDUCATION

Although I slipped through high school, I still managed grades that were good enough to get me admitted to CCNY tuition-free. But the informal, underground, virtual college at New York University overwhelmed the formal stuff at CCNY. It opened my eyes. It let me in on secrets. It challenged all the old assumptions, and, far more than I realized, it formed the basis for how I thought—and how I still think—about everything: business, family, politics. Certainly my distaste for the orthodox, for the view that "this is the way it's done," was incubated there. Why do I think that important? Because it caused and still causes me to think anew. For me, that's crucial. The instinct to come at a challenge de novo, and to do so comfortably, is worth plenty. For most people it is very difficult. They must force themselves to think anew (something like turning on that think switch). NYU taught me to do it naturally, comfortably—almost instinctively. That makes orthodoxy the difficult way, not the easy way. This is not to urge nonconformity for the sake of nonconformity. Rather the urge is to look at every option, including the old familiar way, to refuse to be captive to a process and be open to any answer that is consistent with your compass.

ON DIALOGUE

I make much of the jazz quartet as Harman's central management strength. It is considered by some to be the company's core.

As I described earlier, I first challenged the orthodoxy of top-down command management when confronting the contradictions in my behavior at Friends World College and at Harman's factory in Bolivar, Tennessee, in the early 1970s.

I realized that conversations I had then with Michael Maccoby were different from any I had engaged in with others. They were not discussion or debate in which each of us took and defended our positions. They were rather open explorations of the subject in which we offered our own experience and insights, not for the purpose of prevailing, but to find new ground. Michael brought perspective. I brought puzzlement. We had dialogue.

I discovered then that subordinating myself to the exchange permitted altogether new thoughts to develop, altogether new ideas to generate. It was my awakening to the power of dialogue in business. The Quakers are devoted to consensus. Some may think of it as discussion or debate, which does not end until all have reached agreement. In serious Quaker practice, however, it is a process much closer to dialogue. Each participant presents his own view, but each is committed to patient attention to and consideration of the views of the others. Those with a minority view carry a major responsibility. It is to avoid clinging to that view to the bitter end, to be open to persuasion, and not to unreasonably obstruct resolution. Friends World College was committed to this dialogic process.

The Aspen Institute, on whose board I serve, has a similar view. The Institute believes that the world's most intractable problems can yield to reasonable resolution when competent people engage in dialogue.

Openness to discovery is part of what the social scientist, Daniel Yankelovich, calls "the magic of dialogue." It is what I refer to when I speak of the leader as catalyst, encouraging that dialogue and prompting the generation of something more than any of the participants brought to the meeting. In his excellent book *The Magic of Dialogue*, Yankelovich distinguishes dialogue from debate and discussion. The purpose of debate, he notes, is to win the argument. Dialogue's purpose is to reveal, by accepting the view that a number of people have pieces of the answer, that together they can craft a solution. Dialogue, he states, is also distinguished from discussion, because in dialogue the operating assumption is that all the participants are equal. Further, the participants bring empathy—that ability and readiness to examine one's own assumptions and those of the other participants, to examine and to respond.

All of that echoes my view of the jazz quartet—the ability to listen equably to others and reach for something more than their initial views. This is no small thing. It is the essence of a new kind of leadership and a new kind of corporate management. It is the factor that promises more than the sum of the parts.

I promote dialogue everywhere in our company. It is the central aspect of our board meetings, where we dispose of the nuts and bolts of the business quickly so that we can turn to dialogue about the company, the technology, and the industry. I trace our board's ability to move promptly on major issues to this practice. Management does not engage in merely selling our views to the board. We encourage open exchanges that borrow from the differences in experience around the table, and through it we build trust and the readiness to act.

A great weakness of orthodox administration, especially when headed by an otherwise strong, creative leader, is what I call the "uniflex syndrome." It typifies the operational system in which everything and everybody conspires to reinforce the leader and diminish all others. It inhibits growth and creativity for all except one. In effect, it creates an organization of a single prince and a phalanx of spear-carriers.

Years ago at Bolivar, I assembled our key staff. "Folks," I said, "I have a great idea. We now manufacture several million remote-controlled sideview mirrors for Ford, General Motors, and Chrysler. But we make them the same way we did ten years ago when we produced several hundred thousand. That does not make any sense. The mirror we make now has the same thirty-two discrete parts it always had. Instead of concentrating our energy on producing each of those parts at less cost, I propose that we examine the basic design assumptions of the product and the way in which we assemble the component parts. Why, for example, can't they snap and plug together instead of being screwed or riveted—and why must there be thirty-two parts? Why shouldn't we design, without sacrificing the basic operating system of the mirror, so that we have, let us say, twenty parts? I really haven't thought much about the details, but as an example, every mirror now uses three relatively expensive die castings. One is the base that joins the mirror to the car body. The second is the stem, and the third houses the mirror and connecting cables. Why can't we design a single casting that encompasses the three, provides a new styling opportunity, and, in combination with the reduced number of parts, results in a better, less expensive product? We might give it a name to dramatize the fact that it is an all-new flexible cable-controlled side-view mirror. We might call it Uniflex.

"That's the rough, unpolished idea. I propose that you set up a task force to refine and develop the idea. I won't be surprised if what you present accomplishes my basic purpose, but includes none of my superficial suggestions."

Several months later an artful packaging of everything I had suggested was delivered for my consideration. Handsome color sketches of a single die-cast housing, and a proposed design that reduced the total number of parts from 32 to 20. The new product had some plugging and snapping together, and a flashy new name—Uniflex! Not one original thought had been presented.

Nothing came of the product. But the experience contributed to my awakening. Before the great experiment at Bolivar, we were arranged so that our executives functioned to support and reflect the attitudes of the leader, no matter how incomplete and superficial his ideas. There was no dialogue, only a process that inhibited growth and creativity for all.

More recently I asked a group of our engineers, lawyers, and marketing people to join with our jazz quartet to discuss a problem that was arising from the development of our multifunctional digital systems for the carmakers. The systems rely on software code. They permit, indeed they require, updating on an annual basis to keep current with changes in services or standards in the developing technology, and to assure that the systems are not made obsolete by developments in communications or entertainment.

Our group assembled to define the problem, estimate the additional engineering staff required to deal with it, and consider the new costs such a program would represent. As the dialogue among equals developed, we realized that what each of us saw as a problem at the outset was in fact an opportunity. Rather than thinking of the costs as additional expenses we would be obliged to absorb, we began to see it as intriguing. If instead of waiting until our clients approached us with a new requirement, we approached them early enough so that they could anticipate the need and the cost of updating, we might build a profitable new business. Dialogue at work. Rarely in my experience does such a step occur in traditional meetings conducted by the conventional commander in chief.

ON INTERVIEWING

The job interview is a serious challenge, both to the interviewer and the interviewee. From the perspective of the interviewer, the worst trap is the familiar catechism. That series of questions, framed without consideration for the personality of either participant in the interview, is doomed to failure. If there is one thing I know about interviewing, it is that I don't know how to interview. That may seem to be posturing, but it is not. I mean that one should not use a formulaic, invariable questionnaire as standard procedure. It elicits little more than do the familiar forms one fills out when going for a medical examination. Surely it depersonalizes what is one of the most personal exchanges that ever occurs in business.

The interviewer doesn't have a more important goal than to put the interviewee at ease. Think about it; if we're talking about a position of some consequence, the meeting usually takes place in a setting that is likely to be intimidating to the candidate. Since the interviewer wants to learn as much as possible about the candidate, it makes sense to generate an atmosphere that encourages him to deliver the most he has. There is no one way to make the other person comfortable. Find your own. I have found it useful to declare, "I don't have a clue about how to proceed with an interview. Please help me." When it is practical, I find it very useful to present a real problem and then ask whether there is anything in the candidate's experience that might excite an answer to such a problem.

By the time someone has come to see me, the interviewing process has already determined if the applicant is technically qualified. I can start the conversation with that assumption, and I can therefore proceed on the basis that it is not for me to measure technical competence, but rather to determine just how this person thinks—what tools he uses to deal with a question—how orderly a process he brings to the exchange. Through many experiences I have learned that once the interview is under way, and dealing with reasonably interesting and pertinent material, a conversation happens. A conversation is far better than a catechism.

Nothing leaves me more astonished than the evidence that so many otherwise serious people come to an interview with no preparation. Really, how much trouble is it to learn something about the company and, for that matter, to learn something about the interviewer? I can tell you that were I to be interviewed by Jack Welch, the moment would come when he would hear me say something to the effect, "That is so interesting—I had wondered about that very point when reading chapter 7 of your book. You said of a job candidate, 'The man displayed business vision and edge.' What did you mean by 'edge'?" Whether the substance of the question is crucial or not, there is little doubt that Mr. Welch would respond to the fact that I had read his book and thought about it.

Two types of people always leave a poor impression when they engage in an interview. The first is the chatterbox, the person who really doesn't listen to the other fellow and who goes on endlessly, with no effort to engage in a real exchange. The second is the candidate without curiosity, awareness, or enthusiasm for the job.

I have learned to place little value in references. Sadly, when asked for one, many people take cover. "I don't know the person calling me—why should I run the risk of being quoted, and why should I be the one to compromise an opportunity for the person I do know?" That attitude leads to a diluted or dishonest evaluation. I prefer to depend on my own and my colleagues' assessments.

Similarly, I have found too often that when I am called for a reference, the caller has already made up his mind and is merely going through the motions. On a few occasions, when I have felt obliged to offer a negative evaluation, the response has been "thank you" and the person was hired.

THE ARTS IN BUSINESS

Neither the graphic nor the musical arts should be thought of as cosmetics—something with which to add visual or auditory appeal to the otherwise important elements of life. Unfortunately, in the business world they are thought of that way more often than not.

Add literature, and you have business's great put-down of our richest inheritance. The poets, painters, composers, and writers are the most creative interpreters of the lives we live and the way in which we live them. They reveal how we are and how we got that way—and they reveal where true hope lies.

Sadly, it is commonplace to hear people in business speak of their intention to take some courses, visit some museums—perhaps go to a few concerts—after they retire. The view of the arts as somehow equivalent to volleyball or badminton—something to engage you in your spare time—is unfortunate because it wastes what should be an enormous resource. When seen as organic, as integral to the design of a product or place, the arts become illuminating instruments—surely not material to be left to some outside expert.

Reading, writing, and listening to music become extraordinary tools when you make them part of your active life.

There is a legendary story of a student asking Michelangelo how in the world he had created his miraculous sculpture *David*. Michelangelo replied, in effect, "David was there in the marble all the time. All I did was release him." Albert Einstein once observed, "Mozart's music was always there. It is part of the inner beauty of the universe, simply waiting to be revealed." Each expression identifies a sense of the arts not as cosmetic, not as superficial decoration, but as intrinsic and organic. Those who think of the arts that way find in them an enormously valuable interpretive instrument.

INDUSTRIAL DESIGN

Sadly, industrial design (ID) is still too often seen as cosmetics— "put a pretty dress on the pig." And ID is often a sorry example of Procrustean thought. In the early days of our business, Harman/Kardon did some very bright things with ID. We turned away from old machinery design and made intelligent use of color, materials, and texture.

When the transistor and printed circuit boards arrived in the early 1950s, all electronics manufacturers treated them as a challenge—the wrong challenge—"How do we use these things," they asked, "and not change the appearance of the product?" Our original products had used vacuum tubes and cable harnesses. They were heat producing, bulky, and space demanding. Those elements drove the ID and the products reflected it—they looked as they should. With the arrival of the transistor and the printed circuit board, there was an opportunity to change the physical appearance to reflect the opportunities presented by compactness and reduced heat—and we and every other manufacturer ignored it. The new products looked just like the old. We had all been Procrustes.

With the arrival of the digital age, new opportunities have been presented. Heat, and the bulky heat sinks required to disperse it, have virtually disappeared. The mass of electrical components has been reduced significantly. The time to design products that reflect the new technology is now. Yes, there are constraints; at least for some time, some of the new products must work with some of the old. But that will be temporary.

Apple has shown a rare understanding that the physical appearance of new digital products should reflect the new technology. We're not there yet. We and virtually everyone else have a long way to go. I, for one, am eager to go there.

ON GOLF

Golf is a special, magical affair—unlike anything else I have experienced. I have been in its thrall for almost fifty years. Golf has spawned special friendships. Golf friends are a different breed, cutting across class, race, and position. Everyone who plays is equal, and golf handicaps permit players of any skill level to play, and even compete, with players of any other level.

Stride a fairway as light is beginning to insinuate itself—and you are in Brigadoon. Walk alone, play alone, or go by yourself with a caddy only, and you will know sanctuary.

I played weekend golf as our company was emerging, and it brought me joy and unique friendships. The joy was in hunting the aesthetic of the golf swing. The swing is, at once, stunningly seductive and elusive. I continue to search for its essence, and I am convinced that it rests with Michelangelo, Mozart, and the farmer who whittled away everything that wasn't hoss. Reduce the swing to a sublimely simple, repetitive motion and you will have mastered it. In mastering the swing, you have gone a long way to mastering yourself. I am unlikely ever to get there, but the effort is an act that demands discipline, devotion, and grace. It appeals to me as a metaphor for so much else in life.

If you have any interest in golf at all, you have heard that the master, Ben Hogan, observed that if he made two or three perfect swings in a round of golf—"that was a big deal." I would settle for one such swing a season.

In golf it is critical that you be both relaxed and attentive—a very tough combination. If you are only relaxed, you are certain to make a bad swing. If you are only attentive, you are certain to swing mechanically and therefore unsatisfactorily. That same combination of relaxation and attention is also the critical combination in the pursuit and management of business.

Golf provides me with matchless friendships, stripped of pretense and artifice. Bob Feldman was the perennial club champion at Engineers Country Club on Long Island. We had a friendly bet each time we played. He was the better player then, and gave me extra shots so that we could play "loser buys lunch." No matter how well I might play, the champ always managed to trump me, and I would sign the chit for our lunches. Then came that memorable day when I won, and the club bookkeeper was so puzzled, he felt compelled to telephone the club champ. "Something fraudulent seems to have happened, Mr. Feldman. Someone has charged two lunches to your account."

I need no reminder to think warmly of Bob Feldman, of Don Brown, of George Barnes, and Irwin Edlavitch—men I have been to the sanctuary with, learned from, and been kept young by. This year I added Jane Harman to the list. She is discovering why I call golf magic.

Just today, as I was completing the writing of this book, I received a startling e-mail. It read:

> Dear Dr. Harman:
>
> I am a "blast from your past." Heard a discussion of your company on CNBC the other morning, and I had to write—if for nothing else to thank you for helping to contribute to my personal work ethic, value system, and sense of always striving for excellence—one that seems to still permeate your company today (as evidenced by the stock's performance in recent months).
>
> Specifically, now that your interest has been tweaked, as a teenager I used to caddy for you (and quite often a friend of yours in those days, a Mr. Robert Feldman) at the Engineers Country Club in Roslyn, N.Y., back in the early 1960's.
>
> I came from a family of modest means, but strong in values, and

working with and seeing examples like yourself as a youngster made a lasting impression on me not just to strive to always do my best, but also be considerate to people and to give back along the way—hey, isn't that what life is all about? After all, at the proverbial "end of the day," our personal score card will ultimately be measured by many of these same values.

As a youngster, while recognizing the vast economic gulf which existed between members at the Engineers Club and those of us who were fortunate to carry your golf bag on many occasions, you were genuinely interested in how many of us were doing and what our goals were. Well, now I can tell you, as the first in my family to go to college, earn two masters degrees, and experience a modest degree of success as a public speaker on economic and tax matters, as well as employee benefits, my wonderful wife of nearly 30 years, Linda, and I are retired (but still consulting) and living in Arizona. Moreover, we raised two fine sons, who work and reside back in New England.

Just thought you might like to hear about an example of how we can touch the lives of many along life's journey. Thank you, Dr. Harman.

My best,

Keith E. Forrest

P.S. As I recall, your handicap was about a 10 back in those days. I'll bet if today's technology in golf equipment was available when you played at Engineers in the early 1960's, you'd have been a "5." Certainly, as an example, if my memory serves me correctly, your drives on #1 would have easily carried the dog leg left, and darn near been on the green. You could really hit' em back then, just like you've done in an even more important game—THE GAME OF LIFE!

Keith Forrest's letter affirmed the impact each of us can have on another's life. I thank him in return.

ON LONGEVITY—GRIST FOR MY TREADMILL

In the foreword of this book I stated that I'm eighty-four. Yet I work out every day. I shot my age and better at golf several times this year, and I cannot remember missing a single day at work. And I really love my work. It is creative, demanding, interesting, always new, and very rewarding. I enjoy it far more than my time as deputy secretary of commerce in the Carter Cabinet and more than my time as president of Friends World College. I have lived a long life, birthed six wonderful children and gained another two, inherited as infants, when I married Jane. She, by the way, is a five-term congresswoman and the ranking member of the House Intelligence Committee.

The company is at its historic peak measured in sales, earnings, technological command, and stock price, and I continue, fully engaged, fully responsible, and fully committed.

Because I maintain a vigorous schedule of work and travel, I am often asked for the secret of my longevity. It is not complicated. I am convinced that a combination of appropriate eating, regular exercise, curiosity, and humor has been my source. I work out every day, three times weekly with a trainer. I do many stretching exercises. They are critically important once you pass forty years. I concentrate on flexes and crunches for the abdomen because a strong abdomen is key to posture, to walking, and to the ability to climb up and down stairs easily. I also run several times a week, outdoors if the weather permits, or on the treadmill at home if it does not. I come to every workout with a full agenda in my mind of issues to work through that have been unyielding or inaccessible. It makes the time disappear and eliminates the boredom. I think of the agenda as grist for my treadmill.

It matters less how much of a workout one does and much more that one does it regularly. I know so many men who devote far more attention to the care and cleaning of their automobiles than they do to their one and only body.

If regularity is the key to exercise, discipline is the key to eating: a modest breakfast dominated by fruit, a decent lunch, and a light dinner. The combination of regular exercise and moderate eating is crucial to a long and healthy physical life.

I am convinced that it is humor and curiosity that have kept me young. It never surprises me when I am asked, "Just how old are you?" I invariably respond, "How old do you think I am?" More frequently than not, the answer is "63 or 64 years old." And my rejoinder is, "Does it surprise you to learn that you're wrong by 20 years?" As my respondent looks at me with puzzlement, I explain, "I'm 44."

Part of the folklore in my family is related to my voracious reading. Thirty-five years ago the former governor of Maine and onetime presidential candidate, Ed Muskie, stopped by to visit at my home in New York City. On the coffee table he spied a copy of Edwin Newman's lovely book, *Strictly Speaking*. Edwin Newman was then in his heyday as a television journalist, wit, and commentator. In typical politician fashion, Mr. Muskie looked first to the index. Disappointed that he did not find his name in it, he was ready to discard the book. "Hold on," I said. "Before you toss that book, you should read the inscription." Ed Muskie read the inscription: "To Sidney Harman, who taught me everything I know about the English language. With great admiration. Edwin Newman."

Muskie put the book down and looked at me in awe. "That's very impressive," he said. "It should be," I replied. "I wrote it myself." While Muskie enjoyed the moment, it has become the stuff of legend in my family. Not a birthday, a Father's Day, a Christmas holiday passes without a sweet addition to my extensive library. You, dear reader, should read the inscriptions to me by Churchill, Roosevelt, Kierkegaard, and Voltaire.

I wish I had a collection of products, newspaper clips, memoranda, and other historical artifacts of my long life in business, education, and government. I don't. It never occurred to me that I was doing anything worth preserving in print or product. I urge you not to fall into the same error. Keep a record of what you're doing. It need not be a diary, but preserve the appropriate, relevant memorabilia. I suspect you'll be grateful you did.

Finally, nothing expands the day, the week, the year, or a life like the exquisite excitement of a new idea. Take no day for granted. Keep engaged in some serious activity, always. Retirement is the enemy of longevity. An idea rather than an apple a day. The mind goes first—then the body.

Thirty years ago I received my doctorate in social psychology from the Union Graduate School. The title of my dissertation was "Education and Business—New Directions, New Hope." I concluded it with the observation that through my experience at Friends World College and the writing of the dissertation, I had become aware of my growing consciousness. I acknowledged that I had long felt guilty in my role as businessman, but had come to understand and appreciate that it provided a special opportunity to be an active agent for constructive social change. I pledged myself to reject dogma and rhetoric and to embrace invention, daring, and human development.

Now, thirty years later, it remains my point of view and my commitment.

AFTERWORD

I wrote this book alone. My insistence on doing so caused my splendid editor, Roger Scholl, some initial concern. When I explained that the book would promote the great value of writing for people in the business world, and that I could not therefore turn to a ghostwriter or collaborator, he was quick to say, "Write a chapter or two and I will judge whether you are up to it." When Roger approved my original offering, I was encouraged that I was up to it, and I have done it.

In writing about writing, I have argued that it is an act of discovery, that writers discover what they know by reading what they have written. More than anything, writing this book has caused me to think again about our "digital management" and its future. After all, it is one thing to have an idea, a dream, a theoretical or abstract organizational idea, and it is quite another to create it and then review it in its reality in its personification in the actual operating members.

I have been doing that, and the following paragraphs speak of each of the participants in our jazz quartet.

Frank Meredith is now much more than the chief financial officer for whom the numbers are the essence. For him the numbers are symbols, and symbols don't fly. They are useful for portraying and useful for giving expression to relationships among functions, but the relationships are what really matter—not the symbols. Balancing the balance sheet means nothing if there are offsetting material errors on both sides. Frank looks through the numbers to their real meaning, and that makes him special. To look through them effectively, he must understand the business in its fullest dimensions—and he does. Frank knows the products, he has schooled himself in the technology, and he engages the marketing and manufacturing people with empathetic understanding of their work. And he has become an excellent public speaker.

Gregg Stapleton arrived at Harman International from General Electric. He brought much relevant experience with him, but I believe that he has developed well beyond what he brought—especially so since he became a member of the quartet. Gregg has taken on responsibility for developing third- and fourth-level managers everywhere in the company. He could not do his day job as chief operating officer without deep knowledge of every aspect of our operations. That he has, and I believe that he will ultimately lead Harman International. I am convinced that he would be a far better leader for this company than for any other he might join. After all, it is his company, he has been nurturing and building it. It rewards him well, he learns from it daily, and it has enormous opportunity before it. Why go anywhere else?

Bernie Girod is our solid pilot. He has become the reservoir into which the tributaries of manufacturing, engineering, finance, and planning flow. It is he who by his very nature is the company convenor. I do it because I am convinced that it is right and productive. Bernie does it because it is in his bones. Bernie is my nominee to succeed me as chairman, even as he has already succeeded me in the role of CEO, but each of the others would also qualify. The company would be different in important respects no matter who succeeded me. I believe we have created the core around which a new quartet would quickly coalesce.

I am the resident visionary, but I also pay attention to the details—big-time. Although I am involved in every aspect of our work—the technical and the financial—I take the lead on advertising, industrial design, and strategic planning. But principally I regard myself as guardian of the company's soul. I initiated a program to counter domestic violence. I insist that if we are to have plants in Mexico for Chrysler and in China to engage that market, they must be model plants that provide world-class working environments and world-class engagement in their communities. If that is not their role, they are exploiting the people in those regions, and we reject that role. I accept absolutely the need to control runaway medical benefit costs, but I insist that any new plans must, in the net, provide no less service for our employees. Then I hold meetings to satisfy myself that they do just that. I do all of it because it makes me feel better, but I also do all of it because I am convinced that a company with conscience and soul will prosper over many years.

If the jazz quartet works so well, why not enlarge it? We do enlarge it by pushing its principles of operation deep into the company and by adding to the key group when it seems appropriate. Erich Geiger is, in my view, a technical genius, and he has led the development and growth of our automotive OEM business in Europe. Last year he was asked to manage the consolidation of our American, Asian, and European OEM operations and to become the chief executive of the consolidated group. With that step, Erich has joined the jazz quartet and it will hereafter be a quintet. When he retires from operations, as he plans to after another year in his new role, Dr. Geiger will become the chief scientist of the corporation. In that role, he will offer his experience and his wisdom to the technology people across the span of our company.

In applauding these fellows, I recognize that I am advertising them to the rest of the business world. One might say that I am putting the company at risk of losing them. If they are so good, isn't this an invitation to a headhunter? It may well be, but I do not think that after all this time and the company's success that any of them is a big secret to the rest of industry. I am certain that they are approached frequently. And I know that it would take a very big, very attractive offer to seduce any of them. That big offer cannot be measured in dollars and perks only. There is an intangible and powerful pull in this jazz group. It is not just any jazz quintet; it is not Gregg's or Frank's or Bernie's or Erich's. It is ours. And each must know that he is far less a talent without the others. Each of us has an enormous personal investment in the amalgam and would lose it if he departed.